MORE LEGENDS & FOLKLORE FROM BARRY, BRIDGEND AND THE VALE

GRAHAM LOVELUCK-EDWARDS

WITH ILLUSTRATIONS BY
JESSICA LOVELUCK-EDWARDS

The right of Graham Loveluck-Edwards to be identified as the
Author of the Work has been asserted by him in accordance with the
Copyright, Designs and Patents Act 1988.

More Legends and Folklore from Barry, Bridgend and the Vale
© Text and photographs by Graham Loveluck-Edwards 2022
© Artwork by Jessica Loveluck-Edwards 2022

ISBN: 9978-1-915439-38-3
Printed and bound in the UK by
Severn, Bristol Road, Gloucester, GL2 5EU

Published by
Candy Jar Books
Mackintosh House
136 Newport Road, Cardiff, CF24 1DJ
www.candyjarbooks.co.uk

Dedicated to the memory of Uncle Peter, AKA Peter James.

*My Godfather, childhood mentor,
most learnéd historian, and an amazing storyteller.*

A true Glamorgan legend lost to us in 2022.

CONTENTS

PART II
MYTHS, FOLKLORE AND THE SUPERNATURAL

INTRODUCTION

May I begin by welcoming you to a book I hope you will love, a book packed solid with myths, legends and stories from history, all of them local to the area once encompassed by the ancient kingdom of Glywysing, latterly the county of Glamorgan.

Many erroneously believe this area to have been the kingdom of Morgannwg, but in fact this was a merger of Glywysing and Gwent, and included Monmouthshire and Newport, which are not covered here. In modern terms, our area of interest is Bridgend, Cardiff, Llantrisant and the Vale of Glamorgan.

When I published my first collection of such stories, *Legends and Folklore of Bridgend and the Vale,* I received one comment above all others: 'I didn't think there *was* any history in this area.'

In a way, I guess this is a compliment, suggesting that the book dispelled this notion. However, readers may be surprised anew to learn that the first book barely scratched the surface. Not only was I left with enough stories to fill this second volume, but in writing the book before you now, I have again been forced to leave quite a few out.

That said, I can well understand why this bounty might come as a surprise.

If you walk into a major book shop and ask if they have any books on pre-industrial Glamorgan history, they will look at you as if you have lost your mind. 'Pre-industrial Glamorgan history?' they will ask. 'Isn't that an oxymoron?'

Moreover, pick up a volume of general British history, and you'll do well to find any mention of our neck of the woods before the industrial revolution. Maybe a paragraph on the battle of St Fagans, during the English Civil War, or a few footnotes about castles – but that would be about it.

It would be easy to think that nothing happened here until people discovered iron and coal. Oh contraire.

People have been living and dying, marrying and giving birth, fighting and unifying here since the very earliest moments of British human history. We had all the things that history is made of in abundance: kings and usurpers, battles and wars, heroes and traitors, saints and scoundrels, outlaws and scandals.

Not only this, but once upon a time, we had an incredible wealth of documentation recording these goings on. From the fifth century, this area was of particular spiritual and religious significance. In fact, Llantwit Major is believed to be the birthplace of Christianity in Wales. It was once littered with monastic cells and a couple of major monasteries of the Celtic Church. Before the Tudor period, most historians of note were monks, and these cells and monasteries were staffed by an army of them. For centuries, these chroniclers were busy recording the life and times of our region.

Sadly, countless manuscripts were destroyed by the Norman invaders, who sacked the Celtic Church and replaced it with their own. This was all part of a wider effort of subjugation, an attempt to force the locals to forget their old identity. The Norman invasion of South Wales was a messy affair.

After the Norman conquest, with the exception of Neath, most of our monasteries were demoted to little more than local branches of their English counterparts. Henceforth, contemporary British chroniclers of note, drawn to these more prestigious institutions, predictably focussed on events in England: English courts, English legislature – English history.

Even those aristocrats who claimed the new Welsh conquests as their personal fiefdoms spent little time here. The de Clairs and Beauforts, the earls of Glamorgan, lived out most of their days on estates in other parts of Britain.

There were a couple of notable exceptions. The cartographer John Speed and the 'father of British history' John Leland visited Glamorgan in the sixteenth and seventeenth centuries respectively. They at least give us *some* contemporary commentary. But in the main the recording of our history had to be accomplished in a different way.

That job fell to the bards.

Most of the stories in this book come to us from songs, poems and folklore, captured by ordinary people and re-told across the generations around crackling log fires on cold winter nights. They stem, in the main, from history, but are full of embellishments, exaggerations and questionable interpretations. And some, as you will discover, are purely for entertainment.

Sadly, I cannot take the credit for any of them. They are all the fruits of my research into our glorious and at times dubious local history and folklore.

I have tried to do more than simply re-tell these stories. I have also looked at their origins, examined their likely veracity, and explored their contemporary context. I want this to be more than just an enjoyable storybook. I want it to be a conduit from which we can all learn about our colourful past.

PART ONE

STORIES BASED
ON HISTORY

THE NEMESIS OF
COLYN DOLPHYN

Here's a belting story to kick this book off. It has all the ingredients you could hope for: pirates, aristo-crats, vengeance and a gory murder. And it all centres around a place on our doorstep.

The place in question is Reynolds Cave, on Tresilian Bay, near Llantwit Major. If you don't know it, it is easy to find. Just take a walk from Llantwit Major beach in a westerly direction along the Heritage Coastal Path, in the direction of St Donats Castle and Nash Point.

After roughly half a mile, having meandered along the cliff tops past the remains of a Second World War bunker, the path drops down onto a pebble-strewn beach. This is Tresilian Bay, which takes its name from a third or fourth century Welsh prince called Sylian. His court used to stand somewhere nearby the rather elegant Georgian house that overlooks the beach today.

We do not know a great deal about Sylian, but there are stories that he used Reynolds Cave as a prison. Those who crossed him would find themselves chained up to the rock face in the cave, which floods twice a day with the tide. (Incidentally, the second biggest tidal flow anywhere in the world.)

At this point I feel duty-bound to warn you not to actually go into the cave itself. Be satisfied to look at it from a safe distance. The cliff face here is very brittle, and as the numerous signs in the vicinity warn, there are regular rock falls. Countless people have been injured or killed by ignoring these warnings, so please, I would hate for a reader of this book to suffer the same fate. Especially when, as you are about to discover, this place has seen more than its fair share of death already.

The events I am about to describe took place in the seventeenth century. Back then, Tresilian House was an inn, and a notorious meeting place for pirates, smugglers, ship wreckers and cutthroats of all kinds. In slightly later history, one of its patrons was the infamous Cap Coch, who when he wasn't occupied running his own inn, kept himself busy as a highwayman, bandit, and mass murderer.

It was a far cry from the altogether more genteel surroundings of St Donats Castle, only a mile further west. Here, Sir Edward Stardling and his family lived a life of luxury, civility and religious devotion. But one night in 1649, these two worlds would collide, and the ramifications for all concerned would be monumental.

One of the regular ne'r-do-wells propping up the bar at the Tresilian Inn was Colyn Dolphyn, a pirate who operated out of Lundy, but was originally from Brittany in France. He got a brief paragraph in my first book, *Legends and Folklore of Bridgend and the Vale*.

He was a huge man, well over six feet tall and muscular

and athletic with it. He dwarfed his crew like Saul in Israel, on board his ship the *Sea Swallow*.

Reynolds Cave on Tresilian Bay

In the period between 1500 and 1800, ports in this area were booming. For example Aberthaw, just up the road from Llantwit Major, and these days little more than a couple of hamlets, was at the time a major port. Most of its trade was with ports across the channel, in places like Bristol and Minehead, and various others dotted along the north Somerset and north Devon coast. The many merchant ships passing back and fore across this thin strip of water provided rich pickings for the pirates that combed this coastline. Dolphyn was just one of many in that regard, though because of his size and ruthless reputation, he was one of the most feared.

One night, the *Sea Swallow* was heading back to Lundy after a disappointing day's hunting, when the lookout spotted a vessel leaving Minehead and heading towards the South

Wales coast. It was running low in the water, a tell-tale sign of a heavy cargo, and Dolphyn boomed out to his men to change their course to intercept it.

Pulling up alongside the unfortunate vessel, the pirates boarded with comparatively little resistance, the terrified crew not daring to confront this fearsome mob, who were armed to teeth. Then one of the pirates recognised a passenger: none other than Henry Stradling – soon to become *Sir* Henry Stradling – eldest son and heir of Sir Edward Stradling of St Donats Castle, Lord of St Donats and Chamberlain of South Wales. The young man was travelling with his wife and daughter and some friends, all of whom were wealthy heirs in their own right. They had been to a party in Somerset and were heading back to St Donats.

Knowing the value of these charges was far greater than any cargo, Dolphyn and his men rounded them up, bound them in ropes and blindfolded them, before taking them back to their lair on Lundy. From there, Dolphyn sent a ransom note to the hapless Sir Edward, demanding payment of 2,200 marks for the release of his son Henry and his companions.

2,200 marks was an astonishing sum of money. Sir Edward Stradling was a very wealthy man, but it took him two years to raise the money, and he had to sell his estates in Bassaleg and Rogerstone, in Gwent, to do it.

But once Sir Edward had gathered the funds, both parties to this agreement kept their side of the bargain. Sir Edward paid the ransom and Dolphyn released his son, Henry, and returned him home.

Henry Stradling was absolutely incensed by the whole incident. He already had a reputation as a bit of hot head, but after two years of imprisonment, the desire to exact his revenge on Colyn Dolphyn completely consumed him. He commissioned the building of a watchtower in the grounds of St Donats Castle (the remains of which can still be seen today), and day and night he would sit atop it, gazing out across the sea, waiting for the day that he would spot the sails of the *Sea Swallow* on the horizon. But as days turned into weeks, and months into years, his persistence yielded nothing.

Just as he was starting to wonder whether he had wasted his time, his tenacity paid off. It was dawn, and through the haze of the sunrise, there on the horizon was the *Sea Swallow*. And it seemed to be on a course for Colhugh Beach in Llantwit Major. Henry Stradling ran down into the castle courtyard, summoned together a troop of guards, and they rode down from the castle to intercept Dolphyn.

When they got to the beach, Stradling and his men found Dolphyn's boat and a few members of his crew, but Dolphyn himself was nowhere to be seen. Half the party dismounted their horses and proceeded on foot, to search the woods and coves all around, while the others, knowing the reputation of the Tresilian Inn, headed straight there. They turned the place upside down, questioning all who were present, but Dolphyn was nowhere to be seen. Then one of the regulars mentioned that he had seen Dolphyn running with great haste to Reynolds Cave. The place was well-known amongst smugglers, a useful hiding place that could be accessed by boat at high tide, to offload smuggled contraband, then returned to on foot once the tide had retreated, to collect the booty.

Stradling's men gingerly stepped across the pebbles and boulders strewn along Tresilian Bay and peered inside the cave. There, standing bold as brass, like a giant of the sea, was Colyn Dolphyn. As they advanced to arrest him, he put up quite a fight, leaving some cuts and injuries to remember him by. But as others nearby heard the scuffle and joined in the fight, he was eventually overcome, and was clapped in chains to await Sir Henry, who had a score to settle.

Henry Stradling was grinning from ear to ear as he came upon the subdued pirate. He had a particularly grisly end in mind for his erstwhile captor. He ordered his men to beat Dolphyn until he lost consciousness, then explained his plan.

When the pirate came to, he found himself buried up to his neck in the sand, at the mouth of Reynolds Cave. He was unable to move and scarcely able to breathe. In front of him, a wooden scaffold had been erected. He was helpless other than to watch as the rounded-up members of his crew were hung one by one.

Then Stradling and his men retired beyond the shoreline to watch Dolphyn's final torment. Powerless, the pirate pleaded for mercy as the approaching tide swept closer and closer. Finally, he was engulfed, drowning at the entrance of Reynolds Cave

To this day, on stormy nights at Tresilian Bay, as the tide makes its way in, Dolphyn's ghostly cries for mercy echo around the mouth of the cave, until the waves pass over the point where he died.

A great story, I am sure you would agree. But is any of it true?

Well, we know that all the major players were real people, as there are multiple, contemporary, documented accounts of them. The sales of the Stradling estates in Gwent are also verifiable, and there is even some corroboration of the kidnapping of Harry Stradling and his eventual ransom.

But was Colyn Dolphyn *really* drowned by being buried up to his neck in sand? It does seem an especially brutal mode of execution, although I am afraid to say that does not rule it out. A little later in this book we will be looking at the Glamorgan Plea Rolls, which record what used to go on in the official courts of the Crown. It was an especially brutal age, where the life of a peasant or outlaw did not hold much value in the eyes of the aristocrats who ruled over them. The most brutal modes of execution were often reserved not so much for the worst crimes, but for people who had shown disrespect for their superiors.

There *are* a few question marks, however.

Firstly, there are alternative accounts of his actually having been killed by hanging from a tree in St Donats. Then there is the fact that pirates being buried up to their necks in sand is a bit of a recurring theme in seafaring stories of this era. Of course, that does not necessarily mean that this particular instance didn't happen, but it is a red flag.

'Ah yes,' you might say, 'but I have been to Tresilian Bay, and I couldn't see any sand in front of the cave. It's all pebbles and stone.'

This is true. If you visit Tresilian Bay today, the lack of sand in front of the cave might suggest this mode of execution to be fanciful. However, a very good friend of mine, who has the distinction of being a geologist, reliably informs me that just because there is no sand there today, it does not follow that this was the case 350 years ago. Beach topography is constantly changing.

So never fear, this horrific act of brutality, which took place right on our doorstep, has every chance of being true.

SECRETS OF
EWENNY PRIORY

Ewenny Priory is widely recognised as the finest example of unmodernised Norman ecclesiastical work in Britain. It even captured the imagination of the esteemed artist JMW Turner, whose painting of it now hangs in the gallery at the National Museum of Wales in Cathays Park, Cardiff.

But despite its renown, the priory still holds many secrets. Not least of which is why a place supposedly built to house just twelve monks and a prior is quite so big. And why, given that the principal pursuit of those monks would have been study, scribing and worship, their home is built like a mighty fortress.

It's time to settle the question that has flummoxed visitors to this unique building for centuries. Is this place a priory with fortifications, or a castle with a priory next door?

As is usually the case with historical buildings, the answer depends on what point in history you are asking about. If you look at the remains of the building today, it would be easy to fall into the trap of thinking that the whole thing was built in one go. But in truth it was built in phases over the course of over 200 years. With changing times came changing needs, and over the years the buildings were adapted to accommodate these.

But before we get into all that, it is worth looking at the so-called priory's inception, to investigate the original vision for the place.

Ewenny Priory

The story begins around 1115, in the early days following the Norman conquest of Morgannwg.

Prior to this conquest, the border between Norman Britain and the Welsh lordships had been the river Ogmore. The Bridgend area was something like a wild west frontier town. Norman gains would swiftly be lost again, with land constantly swapping hands between attacker and defender. Lordships and territories ebbed and flowed like the coming and going of the tide. Even after the Normans tightened their grip on the area, things didn't really settle down until the reign of Edward I, and that was two hundred years later.

To hold ground as far as the Ogmore took a gargantuan effort and some formidable defences, and I have a theory that Ewenny Priory was originally intended to support in this defence. In my view, the ecclesiastical element only came about due to an intervention – political pressure from someone you might be surprised to find taking an interest in our humble neck of the woods.

The Norman building work at Ewenny Priory was started by William de Londres, one of the legendary Twelve Knights of Glamorgan. He was the lord of Ogmore Castle, a very ambitious man who was not altogether satisfied by the fact that, despite his title, he was still answerable to the Earl of Glamorgan. He moved his interests west, where he could be overlord of all he surveyed, and established the lordship of Kidwelly. It was his son, Maurice, who undertook the majority of the building work in Ewenny.

Even by the standards of other Norman knights, Maurice de Londres was a brute. His fearsome reputation was dramatically encapsulated by his decapitation of the captured Princess Gwenllyan of Dehaubarth in Kidwelly. He was certainly not known to be a godly man. But he was a great military tactician. I believe that he intended to build a castle in Ewenny to provide the local Norman lordships with what scholars have ever since described as a 'quadrilateral defence' of the main crossing points of the Ewenny and Ogmore rivers, with Coity and Newcastle to the north, and Ogmore and Ewenny to the south.

So what persuaded him to instead build what we still describe today as a priory, a place fundamentally intended as a house of God?

It is a commonly held belief that de Londres built the priory to atone for his former sins, just as Richard de Grenville did when he financed the abbey in Neath. It was a bit of a thing amongst Norman knights. They were ultimately God-fearing people, but their vast wealth and power had been amassed largely through ignoring those inconvenient 'thou shalt not kill' and 'thou shalt not steal' bits of the Bible. With that came a certain amount of guilt.

This theory is lent further credence by the principle of Noblesse Oblige, which was popular among the Norman aristocracy. This dictated that, as lords and masters, they had a duty to provide for the well-being of their subjects, at least to some extent. This would have included providing for their spiritual well-being.

But I am not thoroughly convinced. I believe de Londres' real motivations weren't honourable principles, but fear and self-interest. A decree issued by Pope Honorius II himself, dated 12th April 1128, threatened de Londres that if he did not 'restore and make good whatever lands, tithes, obligations, or other valuables he had appropriated from his mother church' then he would be excommunicated.

Maurice de Londres' past was catching up with him.

As I mentioned in my introduction, the Normans did not just invade Wales, they also oversaw the annihilation of the Celtic Church. During the invasion of Morgannwg, de Londres had plundered and destroyed the Christian foundation in Llandaff, and now the Pope wanted him to make good what he had done. And when a twelfth-century Pope wanted something, you did it. Excommunication was seen as the worst punishment that could befall a man. It not only meant social disgrace in life, but that you would be barred from entering Heaven upon your death. Unthinkable.

Faced with such a threat, De Londres might have thought twice about building a castle on a site where many contemporary documents record a pre-existing monastic cell.

Ewenny had been of spiritual significance even before Christianity came to our shores. According to the *Ravenna Cosmography*, which was published in the seventh century, it had been the site of a vision of the Celtic pagan spring goddess Aventi. Any linguists reading will no doubt have picked up on how close 'Aventi' and 'Ewenny' are to each other phonetically.

Then the twelfth-century *Book of Llandaff* lists an '*Ecclesia de Euenhi*' somewhere in the vicinity, likely to be a monastic cell dedicated to the early Welsh saint Eguenni (Eguenni being another possible root of the name Ewenny). We also know that the area was the site of an early shrine commemorating Saint Illtyd.

During the sixth century, around the time Saint Illtyd founded the Cor at Llantwit Major, local monasteries suffered frequently from raids led by marauding Irish pagans. As a former warrior himself, Saint Illtyd was quite capable of leading a spirited defence, and it was maybe this that marked him out as the target of a pagan Irish king, who decided to make hunting down and killing this troublesome saint a personal priority. Illtyd fled for his life, pursued across the Vale by the barbaric rabble, and took refuge in a cave on the banks of the Ewenny River. Here he lived the life of a hermit.

(I must confess that I have heard a rather less exciting version of this story, where instead of being pursued by killer Irishmen, Illtyd was simply pursuing solitude to lose himself in contemplative prayer.)

Unable to leave the cave for fear of Irish warriors, St Illtyd faced almost certain starvation. Then in a dream he saw a host of angels, coming down from heaven with food and water to sustain him. When he woke in the morning, it was all set out at his feet. The angels had saved his life. This divine room service continued until the raiders had withdrawn and Illtyd was able to return to the monastery.

When the first Norman church in Ewenny was consecrated, by Bishop Urban of Llandaff on 29th September 1120, it was dedicated to St Michael 'and all angels' – this 'all angels' bit in reference to St Illtyd's miracle.

De Londres was not the sort of man to let all this religious history sway his decision making. However the threat of excommunication was something different: a social disgrace from which a nobleman could not recover. Any fort-building plans he might have had were scaled back, the only hint of his original ambitions being some defences sufficient to maintain a detachment of men at arms.

De Londres turned the priory over to the Benedictine order of St Peter at Gloucester Abbey, but it seems that the idea of a castle on the banks of the Ewenny survived him. The majority of the fortifications we can see today were built long after his death, in eras when the site was in ostensibly far more pious hands.

However, this is hardly surprising. De Londres knew his strategy, and the priory was excellently located to project military power.

It was during the reign of King Edward I that the majority of the defences to be seen today were built. By this time the priory was flagging as an institution, so there was little resistance to the notion of extending the battlements to the extent we see today. Edward was tired of the troublesome

Welsh continually rising up against the English Crown and had decided to crush the Welsh lordships in West Wales once and for all. Troops were stationed at Ewenny Priory to assist with that campaign.

Not only did the site survive as a fortress for at least another 200 years after this, the evidence seems to suggest it was a fortification of some significance. When Owain Glyndŵr laid siege to Coity Castle in 1405, King Henry IV mustered his troops and launched his counterattack from Ewenny Priory. Afterwards, he nominated the prior, Hugh Morton, to be appointed the next abbot of St Peter's, Gloucester, a huge promotion.

I am quite proud to be able to add one final piece to this chapter, to say that some of Ewenny Priory's secrets were revealed to us by one of my own ancestors, an architect, councillor and historian from Bridgend known as Edward 'Ned' Loveluck. He discovered a long-lost stone sundial in the grounds of the priory, featuring engravings marking out the times of all its services, Mass and calls to prayer. It gives us a very rounded view of the daily routines of the priory's inhabitants, and it is still available to view on site. In that respect, it is the only one of its kind in Wales.

A ROAD THROUGH MILLENNIA: THE ANCIENT GLAMORGAN RIDGEWAY

Between the counties of Bridgend and Rhondda Cynon Taff, there is a bank of rather dramatic and beautiful mountains and hills. Their ruggedness contrasts sharply with the lush green pastures of the lowland coastal areas to the south, known to the ancient Welsh as Y Fro, but these days more commonly referred to as the Vale of Glamorgan. Meandering across the top of this row of peaks is an ancient road, now little more than a footpath. It is known as the Glamorgan Ridgeway.

The Ridgeway predates any other recognisable thoroughfare in the area, even the Via Julia Maritima, a Roman road from the Antonine period, the route of which is these days loosely followed by the A48. The Romans themselves described the Ridgeway as 'ancient', so we can only guess at how long travellers have trod its spectacular path.

In its entirety it runs from the Preseli Mountains in Pembrokeshire to the Severn Estuary. And that's at a minimum. There is evidence to suggest that, during the Roman era, it was still possible to ford the River Severn at low tide, so it could be argued that the road led all the way to London.

The stretch that runs closest to us rises at Margam, Llangeinor, Blackmill, Llantrisant, Mynydd-y-Garth and Caerphilly Mountain. It rewards the intrepid walker with spectacular views over our counties, and across the Bristol Channel to the north Somerset coast. On a clear day you can see as far as the two Severn bridges to the east and the Gower Peninsular to the west.

The Ridgeway is littered with mementoes to its ancient past, to people and settlements come and gone, and to the ways people used to live. It boasts a couple of natural wonders too. One of my favourites is the remains of a petrified forest in the valley above Blackmill. This bank of gnarled and twisted dwarf oak trees would not look out of place in the grounds of Hogwarts, or outside Dracula's castle in a Hammer Horror film.

Also the stuff of gothic horror are the various ruins and abandoned villages strewn along the Ridgeway. Some of the most historically significant are the ruins of Llanbedr-ar-y-Mynydd, also known by its Latin name of St Peter-Super-Montem. These lie on the southern bank of the path, on a triangulation between Brynna, Llanharan and Hendreforgan. Very little is known about this place, other than it was once a thriving community, at its peak around the fifth and sixth centuries. Many believe that the remains of St Peter's Church here are all that is left of one of the first Christian churches ever built in Wales.

According to *Wales Online*, back in 1990, some amateur archaeologists discovered on this site an ancient axe, a knife and a small cross with the inscription '*Pro Anima Artorius*', meaning 'For the Soul of Arthur'. These finds closely followed claims that a memorial stone to King Arthur had been discovered at St Peter's, and speculation was rife that Arthur might actually be buried somewhere around this spot.

Llanbedr-ar-y-Mynydd

Authorities on Arthur's final resting place, such as Geoffrey of Monmouth, generally described it as a place called Avalon: an island beyond a glassy-still sea, abundant in orchards and fruit trees, and ruled over by an enchantress called Morgen. Putting the clues together, it seems most likely to have been the Isle of Mann – but here, tantalisingly, was potential evidence of something closer to home.

A team of professional archaeologists wanted to verify these finds, but their original finders refused access. The professional team conducted a dig of their own but were unable to find anything to support the claims. As much as I would dearly love to tell you that the mythical site of Avalon is on our doorstep, chances are that this was just another ruse to cash in on Arthur's enduring appeal.

Fortunately there are many other, altogether more verifiable tombs up on the Ridgeway. At several points (with the best-known examples being on the summit of the Garth) you will find barrows and cairns (ancient burial sites) from the Bronze Age. The burial mounds on the Garth date back to around 200 years BC, and are evidence of a once-thriving hilltop community. Findings here suggest that the Garth was a sacred site for the Celts, revered as a place of worship – something the early Christians were keen to capitalise on when they arrived, just like they did in Ewenny.

In the sixth century, Saint Cadoc established churches and monasteries throughout the Vale of Glamorgan, most notably the Clas in Llancarfan. He also founded the church in Pentyrch, on the foot slopes of the Garth, as part of a monastic colony. The church is still dedicated to him to this day, as is the well that traditionally gave the village its water supply. The well was believed to have magical healing powers, and as Cadoc is the patron saint of skin conditions and burns, one has to assume that these were the sorts of conditions its waters were most effective at healing. As a result, Pentyrch was an early place of Christian pilgrimage in Wales.

In the valley below is another well of even greater repute: the thermal spring at Taffs Well, where heated water rises through cracks in the limestone in much the same way as in Bath, or Hotwells in Bristol. Taffs Wells' springs have been in use since they were first discovered by the Romans, the water here maintaining an average of 65-66 degrees Fahrenheit regardless of air temperature or time of year, and gushing at the substantial rate of 800 gallons per hour.

For the past 2000 years or so, the Ridgeway has predominantly been used as a drovers' pass. In its earlier days, the lowlands of the Vale were very marshy, and in the winter months would frequently flood. The Ridgeway was the only road from east to west where you could trudge your merry way without getting your feet wet. Even after good roads across the lowlands had finally been established, the toll roads of the nineteenth century saw drovers returning to their traditional routes, to avoid the hefty tolls that were being levied on the turnpikes along the route of the Via Julia Maritima further south.

Drovers were very hardy men. They lived an especially spartan lifestyle, frequently sleeping on open grassland or under hedges, and risking life and limb driving their valuable charges of cattle from the farms of West Wales to the cattle markets of Smithfields in London. The unmissable approach of their herds left them at the mercy of every bandit along the way. A gang of ne'r-do-wells from the Llynfi valley, calling themselves the Red Goblins, are recorded as mounting an ambush on Carmarthenshire drovers walking our stretch of the Ridgeway, and helping themselves to their entire herd. They were presumably not the only gang to strike it big in this way.

In the long history of the Ridgeway, its pathways have also been trod by personages slightly more esteemed than the Red Goblins. In fact, it has a link to one of the most momentous events in British history.

Usurping a throne is a tricky business. Kings liked to perpetuate the notion that they had been personally appointed by God, therefore assuring themselves of a bit of security while on the throne. So when William the Conqueror invaded in 1066, taking the English throne for himself, he was eager to shore up his claims to have been acting within God's will.

That was a tall order: war is not a particularly godly business. William had to grasp at anything he could. For example, in the Bayeux tapestry there is a scene that shows King Harold visiting William in Normandy before the Norman invasion. He is depicted swearing upon holy relics that he recognises William as the legitimate heir to the English Crown.

Another tale went that, during the Battle of Hastings, soldiers in William's army saw visions of some of our ancient Welsh saints. If these saints were on William's side, then clearly there was some ancient precedent supporting the Norman's claims. After all, King Harold, of Saxon descent, was a bit of a Johnny-come-lately when it came to Britannic thrones.

To cement this story, one of the first things William did as king of England was to head out on a pilgrimage to the shrines of these saints. This meant taking the Ridgeway to the tomb of St David, in what today is the cathedral that takes his name, in Pembrokeshire.

Along the way, he also stopped in Newport, at the shrine of the somewhat lesser-known St Woolos the Bearded. St Woolos, it seemed, was a particularly ardent Norman supporter: he had been spotted physically fighting alongside the Norman forces. To be fair, he had always been an unusual saint, as we shall explore in a later chapter.

As the newly crowned William made this pilgrimage over

the Ridgeway, he was accompanied by a young Robert Fitzhamon. It was while on this pilgrimage that Fitzhamon first saw the fertile fields of Morgannwg, spread out before him as he passed along the overlooking hills. Only eleven years later, he would invade these lands, bringing them under the control of the English Crown.

Fitzhamon's legacy is problematic to say the least. But he did at least furnish me with ample material for this book, having stirred up the trouble at the heart of so many of the stories to come.

LEGENDS OF THE
TUBERVILLES

ack in 1571, one of the Vale of Glamorgan's most
famous sons, Sir Edward Stradling (father of Sir Harry
Stradling, kidnapped in our first chapter), wrote and
published an account of the Norman conquest of South Wales.
For over 100 years it was generally accepted as the principal
authority on the subject. These days the pithily titled *The
Winning of the Lordship of Glamorgan out of Welshmens' Hands* is
better known as *The Legend of the Twelve Knights*, and its
historical merit is thought to be dubious. But it contains some
lovely stories.

As mentioned in the previous chapter, during his
pilgrimage to St Davids, William the Conqueror was believed
to have been accompanied by Robert Fitzhamon, eventual
conqueror of South Wales. Well, Fitzhamon also brought
some friends along, including one of his right-hand men, Sir
Payne Tuberville.

Tuberville, like the frustrated mastermind of Ewenny
Priory, William de Londres, was one of the legendary Twelve
Knights of Glamorgan. While on this pilgrimage, Tuberville

would have had a clear view of his future home. At its closest point, the Glamorgan Ridgeway passes through part of the old lordship of Coity (between Heol-y-Cyw and Blackmill), only a couple of miles away from where he would later build his castle.

When Fitzhamon subdued the Welsh, he gave lands and estates in the area to his favourite knights. They were allowed to build castles, keep men at arms, raise taxes and generally keep the native Welsh in check. And if they managed to enlarge their estates by invading neighbouring lands, then good for them.

But the story goes that, for reasons which are not clear, Sir Payne de Tuberville was the exception. He had fought alongside Fitzhamon in the invasion but had fallen out of favour with his master. Instead of receiving estates in return for his service, he was instead sent out to claim his own.

Undaunted, and perhaps thinking back to his travels with his fellow Normans, Tuberville arrived at Coity, where he was met by the incumbent Welsh lord, known as Morgan Gam, or Morgan ap Meurig.

Morgan was part of the same royal bloodline as the deposed king of Morgannwg, Iestyn ap Gwrgan, an asset that he intended to make the most of. He stood before Payne's ranks with a sword held aloft in his left hand, and his daughter Sybil's hand in his right. He instructed Tuberville that if he wanted to lay claim to these lands, he needed to choose whether he would do so by the sword or through marriage to Morgan's daughter.

The Norman knight chose the path of peace and unity and agreed to marry Sybil, and thus became lord of Coity.

*

It is a lovely story, but I suspect that reality might have been an altogether more brutal affair. De Payne's first castle at Coity was a wooden motte and bailey, built on the remains of a Romano-Celtic defensive outpost; however, it was quickly rebuilt and reinforced with stone, better to repel the frequent Welsh raids. In other words, it seems local relations were not quite so peaceful as the tale implies.

Coity Castle today

Sir Edward Stradling may well have been a scholar of history, but he was not one to put such petty concerns as the truth in the way of a good story. In fact, he told some real whoppers.

One of his most glaring fibs was the claim that his own family, the Stradlings, had fought alongside Fitzhamon, and that his estate at St Donats Castle had been gifted as a reward for the family's contribution to the Norman conquest. In reality, the Stradlings did not arrive in Wales until 200 years later, and when they did it was from Switzerland, rather than Normandy.

It seems likely the Tubervilles were also on the receiving end of Stradling's creative imagination. But to give Sir Edward the benefit of the doubt, while any era of peace, harmony and brotherly love between the Normans and the Welsh is almost certainly fiction, with their marriage into the Welsh aristocracy, the Tubervilles did mark themselves out as different from all the other Norman lords. Their Welsh holdings were acquired not through conquest, but through the union of noble lines. Their contemporaries didn't bother with such niceties: they had the Welsh lords slaughtered and took their land for themselves.

But this questionable episode is just the first in a long tradition of the Tubervilles blurring the lines between their Anglo/Norman roots and their adopted Welshness. The family are frequently portrayed in folklore as siding with the Welsh against their fellow countrymen. There are stories of them fighting with Welsh lords against Norman lords, and even suggestions that they fought on the side of Owain Glyndŵr against Henry IV.

It is difficult to say whether there is any truth to their reputation. These stories go somewhat against the grain of what we know of the family's early history.

For example, after the death of Gilbert 'the Red' de Clare at the Battle of Bannockburn, King Edward II appointed the Tubervilles as administrators of Glamorgan. They earned a horrific reputation for forcing taxes and tithes out of starving Welsh peasants at the time of the great famine. So great was their cruelty that it motivated Prince Llywelyn ap Gruffydd to

THE IMPOSTER
OF ST DONATS

Back in the eighteenth century, it was very fashionable for the young bucks of aristocratic families to set off on 'the Grand Tour'. This was a whistlestop tour around Europe, ostensibly to visit the cultural capitals of the world, and broaden their knowledge of art and literature. And of course, to sow their oats. Enough of these refined young gents returned home riddled with syphilis, their inheritances squandered at a gaming table, to give away what really went on.

We have already come across one of the families involved in this story several times, both in this book and its predecessor. The Stradlings, lords of St Donats Castle and one of the most powerful dynasties in Welsh history. Their tenure at St Donats stretched over 600 years, beginning all the way back in the thirteenth century. They were at the height of their power in the Tudor period, despite the fact that, throughout the Reformation, they remained ardently Catholic. This was a choice that saw plenty of other families fall from grace and lose their estates. It is a testament to their power and standing that, despite refusing to convert to the Anglican Church, they continued to hold high office even during the reign of Elizabeth I.

But if their power had not been impacted by the Reformation, it was starting to wane by the end of that other great leveller of British history, the English Civil War. The Stradlings were Royalists, and as such found themselves on the losing side. Three members of the family had fought for the Crown at the Battle of St Fagans, and after defeat there, they were forced into exile as traitors. The gradual decline of the family had begun.

The Stradling relevant to our story is Sir Thomas Stradling, who in the 1730s, when he was in his twenties, planned to go on the Grand Tour with his close friend from university, Sir John Tyrwhitt, the fifth baronet of Stainfield. Tyrwhitt was a wealthy heir in his own right, as well as a very prominent politician. He served as an MP from 1715 to 1734 and was a mover and shaker within the Whigs, the political party which later became the Liberal Party.

Before the two young gentlemen set out on this great adventure, they made a pact with each other. If either was to die while on this tour, then the other would inherit the estate of the deceased. Or so it was claimed.

You can probably guess what happened next.

While the young men were both away, news reached the Stradling family at St Donats that, on the 27th September 1738, while in Montpellier in the south of France, Sir Thomas Stradling had been killed in a duel. The family were devastated. Arrangements were made to bring Sir Thomas' body home, and it was laid in state at St Donats Castle.

But this was just the beginning of their woes.

According to folklore, Sir Thomas Stradling's nurse, who had raised him since he was a baby, wished to pay her respects. She was invited to see his body in one of the state rooms at the castle. Gliding across the dimly lit room in which the coffin stood, she raised the lid to hold the hand of her young charge one last time. But as she reached inside the coffin, she gasped, stopped short, turned and made a sharp exit.

She was convinced that the man in the coffin was not Sir Thomas. It was an imposter. She knew that, as a small boy, Sir Thomas had lost a finger on his left hand; it had been bitten off by (of all things) a donkey. But the man inside the coffin had all his fingers intact.

Gossip was rife on the subject, and for years afterwards, locals visiting St Donats Church would point at Sir Thomas' tomb and declare, 'That is where the imposter lies.'

Sir Thomas had left no heir (always a worry for aristocratic families of the time), but before making his verbal agreement with Sir John Tyrwhitt, he *had* written a will. In it, he had left the castle and his entire estate to his cousin, Bussey Mansel, the 4th baron of Margam. It was said, however, that Bussey had visited St Donats Castle after Sir Thomas' death, where he had been confronted by the ghost of one of the Stradling ancestors. The ghost had declared that it would never countenance the castle passing to a Mansel, and that if Bussey were to enforce the will, then he would be haunted into madness.

Bussey Mansel turned his horse and fled as fast as it would carry him, never again to return to the castle. It is worth pointing out that, despite the family link, Bussy Mansel was a Presbyterian and Parliamentarian who had fought on the side of Cromwell at St Fagans.

The tomb of the last Stradling. Or is it…

It would be nice to believe that this property dispute was settled by a ghost, but in reality it became one of the most protracted and expensive courtroom battles of its day. It remained in litigation for over sixty years, a commentator at the time of the eventual judgement quipping, 'The matter has been resolved so that the Stradlings take a third, the Tyrwhitts take a third, and a third goes to the lawyers.'

Ultimately, however, St Donats Castle did pass to the Tyrwhitts, much to the dismay of the people of St Donats. In fact, it is claimed that the vicar of St Donats Church was so incensed that 'in his fury' he destroyed a windmill and two watermills.

That's a lot of fury for a village parson. It's always the quiet ones you've got to watch.

HALLOWEEN AND ITS LOCAL ORIGINS

Every year, when I see kids dressed up as pumpkins, collecting sweets from random strangers, I ask myself the same question: how on earth has Halloween managed to morph into some innocent, child-friendly celebration?

For our Welsh ancestors, Halloween, or at least the festival that today's tradition is based on, was the single darkest and most ominous day of the year. It started out as a Celtic pagan fire festival called Samhain, and like all Celtic festivals, it was observed devoutly here in South Wales.

Samhain was held at the midpoint between the autumn equinox and the winter solstice, and marked the end of the months of plentiful sunlight and harvest and the beginning of the dark season. The Celts believed that this was the most dangerous time of year, a time when the usual barriers separating the spirit and mortal worlds broke down, leaving the living vulnerable to hauntings, possessions and attacks by malevolent demons. Some even heralded it as the likely point of the end of the world, with only the specific year an uncertainty.

For the Celts, this was no mild, abstract danger. Samhain marked a time of absolute terror, and it called for a mammoth, co-ordinated effort to keep themselves safe.

To empower themselves against this annual threat, the Celts would light huge bonfires with a blazing wheel (a pagan symbol of the sun), maintaining a bright light to beat the shadows back. Then they would sacrifice bulls and cocks, leaving the sacrifices on burial mounds as gifts for their dead ancestors. If there was going to be a war with invading ghosts, demons and spirits, the living Celts wanted to make sure that their own ancestors would fight on their side.

The ceremonial side of things was led by the druids, who would dress up as various gods and dance around the fire. One was Apona, god of horses; another the wild black boar without a tail that represented the god Moccus, known in Welsh as Yr Hwch Ddu Gwta. Moccus was always accompanied by a headless woman, and there is every possibility that this role would have been played by an actual decapitated female corpse. After all, the object of this performance was for the community to make as terrifying a display as possible, to scare away the evil spirits.

This ceremony carried on continuously for three days, and everyone had to participate. By unquestioned agreement, tribes that were at war had to suspend hostilities, putting their differences aside until the end of the festival, to make sure nothing got in the way. Failure to take part was punishable by death.

At the end of the three days, if everyone was alive and not possessed by spirits, it was clear that the alliance between the living and the dead had once again been victorious over the spirit world. Which called for a drink.

The next six days were one great celebration, featuring a great feast with places set for both the living and the dead. Women folk would chatter into the air, to bring the dead up to date with everything that had happened through the year, and the atmosphere of relief and triumph fuelled a bacchanal of drinking and merrymaking.

This double-handed ritual was universal across ancient Britain, although there were a few traditions that were unique to us in South Wales. For example, at the end of the opening three-day ceremony, men would hurl burning logs at each other in a violent game of chicken. All in good fun.

A light against the darkness

Samhain was a really big deal to the ancient Celts, and its significance was massively underestimated by the early Christians. The Church wanted to stamp out all pagan practices that could not be re-branded, and it was hard to see a way of spinning Samhain into something in line with their teachings. They attempted to bring this practise to an end – unsuccessfully.

In the fifth century, Pope Boniface tried the idea of a festival in May, where bonfires would be lit in homage to saints and martyrs. But his idea did nothing to assuage the ancient Britons' fears of invasion from the spirit world at the end of October. So in the ninth century (no rush then – only took 400 years) Pope Gregory moved All Saints Day (known in old English as All Hallows Day) to 1st November. The name 'Halloween' comes from 'All Hallows Eve' – in other words the day before All Saint's Day.

Perhaps recognising that Samhain's week-plus blowout required a little more than a single day's replacement, for the 2nd of November, Gregory also created All Souls Day, when Christians leave offerings on the graves of dead ancestors. Common people found this a bit easier to swallow, but for centuries to follow continued to mark both occasions with bonfires. Eventually the traditional bonfire fell back a few days in the calendar, to commemorate the foiling of the Gunpowder Plot. We still run with that one, meaning that to this day the first week of November, featuring both Bonfire Night and Halloween, retains something of the Samhain flavour.

Many texts observing Welsh life note that, while our ancestors were God-fearing people, they nevertheless maintained many paganistic rituals. As recently as the beginning of the twentieth century, after church on a Sunday, it was common to see the children of a community joining hands in a circle and dancing and singing around the ancient yew trees in the churchyard.

It might sound a bit creepy now, but you could have observed this in pretty much every village in the Vale of Glamorgan, certainly within the lifetime of my own grandparents. This was a tradition dating back thousands of years.

So it will come as no surprise that, even after the rebrand of Samhain, we in Wales maintained a host of traditions that would have had Pope Boniface spinning in his grave. For example, it was still believed that, as autumn turned to winter, one should guard against the magic leaking out of the underworld. This magic was believed to travel through conduits such as ivy, and touching ground ivy around Halloween was thought to give you nightmares.

Moreover, if a boy placed ivy under his pillow on Halloween night, he would see visions of the future in his dreams. A girl would need to grow a rose around a hoop and place that under her pillow to achieve the same.

Then there was the tradition of Coelcerth, which would see the people of the community writing their name on stones and placing them on the Halloween fire – either a bonfire or the household hearth. If by the morning any of the stones were missing, then that person would not live out the year. It was also considered lucky to collect ashes from the Halloween fire and place them in your shoes (although obviously it was not quite so lucky if you didn't wait for them to cool down first).

But before you did so, you'd better make sure to cover up all the mirrors. It was feared that if you looked into a mirror on Halloween, you might see witches staring back at you.

Even that might be the least of your worries if you lived by the sea, however. Tied to the pagan tradition of the dead rising, it was a commonly held belief that on the night of the Samhain (and more latterly Halloween) all the drowned of the sea would rise up out of the water, and ride though the waves on white horses towards the shore. On arrival on the beaches, they would indulge in great revelries. Hence villagers around Nash Point in the Vale of Glamorgan referring to white breakers as 'merry dancers'. To protect themselves against evil spirits, coastal dwellers would hang a sprig of seaweed in the back kitchen of their cottages.

Less sinister were the Cyffel Cynhaeaf, or Harvest Mares. Corn dollies were traditional across Britain, but these were a variation in the shape of a horse. They were central to a peculiar tradition which saw the men of the house trying to hang their handmade Cyffel Cynhaeaf above the hearth. It was the job of the women of the house to make a token effort at preventing them. How to do so? Well, naturally, a water fight. Ultimately the men had to be allowed to win. A metaphor for so much of life, right, sisters?

I know what you're thinking though. Where do pumpkins come in?

In the Middle Ages, a long time after the Celtic tradition had been absorbed into the Christian calendar, another hangover of the old pagan beliefs clung stubbornly on. If a farmer wanted to protect his family from evil witches and fairies, he should burn a bonfire near his farm; but rather than dress up as scary characters and dance around the flames, he and his family should instead hollow out turnips and parsnips, carve scary faces on them, and backlight them with candles. These were called Jack-o-Lanterns.

When people started emigrating to America, they brought this custom with them. They quickly found American pumpkins a lot easier to hollow out than turnips and parsnips, and so the practice of pumpkin carving that we know today was born.

This still doesn't explain how Halloween ended up so child-friendly though. Perhaps it is the influence of Hispanics, and their own traditional celebration on the 1st November, the Day of the Dead. This is a much less frenzied and altogether more friendly affair than a Welsh Samhain, and sees its celebrants creating family altars and heading off to the cemeteries to have huge family picnics around the graves of their descendants.

For all Halloween's deep roots within our culture, the growth of its modern incarnation has been astonishing. I can say with hand on heart that, in the UK, even as recently as the 1980s it just wasn't a thing. Bobbing for apples was about as far as it went.

Perhaps it's time to reclaim the tradition and return it to its origins. Next time Halloween rolls around, don't dress up as Dracula and daub fake cobwebs all over your house. Instead, light a massive bonfire in your garden, scatter dead animals all round your local graveyard, and dance around with the headless corpse of a woman. I'm sure your neighbours will appreciate that you are simply being a purist.

IANTO FRANK, THE HAPLESS HIGHWAYMAN

A contemporary of the legendary Glamorgan outlaw Cap Coch, but nothing like as successful in his dastardly doings, the hapless Ianto Frank was probably more misunderstood than anything else. Certainly the story of his death has been; it is commonly misattributed to his more eminent contemporary. Unfortunately for Ianto's criminal ambitions, there the similarities end.

Ianto lived in the pretty little village of St Hilary, on the edge of Stalling Down, near Cowbridge, and was a regular old soak at the Bush Inn, which is still open today.

The crossroads on Stalling Down were a notorious black spot for bandits and highwaymen. The people of the county even went to the lengths of erecting some gallows there, in the hope that the sight of a hanged felon might dissuade others from following the same path. But to no avail. The robberies continued unabated.

The extent to which Ianto was involved in these crimes is

unclear. You get the impression that he was just an opportun-
istic petty criminal. But after downing a few pints in the Bush,
he would swagger about, boasting that he was the ringleader
of these cutthroats, and warning his fellow patrons to pay him
more respect than they evidently did.

No one really took him very seriously, but his boasting
came back to haunt him when he was caught stealing a sheep.
When he was brought before the magistrate, a question was
asked about his character. First a solitary hand was raised in
the court room. Then another, and another. Suddenly all of
the stories he had been telling at the Bush started to come out:
his dastardly exploits on the downs, the countless victims he
had robbed at the point of a pistol or a sword, and so on.

Seeing where all this was going, Ianto bleated anxious
denials, offering explanations from the dock, only to be
silenced by the magistrate, who now believed he had before
him the mastermind behind the entire criminal blight on the
county. He passed sentence that Ianto 'be hung by the neck
'till he be dead at Pant-Y-Lladron' ('thieves' hollow' in Welsh)
– in other words, the gallows on Stalling Down.

But when the bailiffs of the court came to take him down,
Ianto surprised them all with a sudden burst of athleticism. He
leaped out of the dock and into the courtroom (the lesser hall
at Cowbridge Town Hall), running like a gazelle through the
open door and out into the street. By the time the bailiffs had
got to the door themselves, he was gone. Vanished from sight.

A search party was assembled and went door to door in
Cowbridge and the surrounding villages of Llanblethian, St
Hilary and Aberthin. But Ianto was nowhere to be found. Next
they turned their attention to hedgerows and farm buildings,
and the glades on Stalling Down. Eventually he was discov-

ered hiding in a cave on the edge of a small wooded area near St Hilary. He was dragged out kicking and screaming, and made to face the hangman. When asked for some last words, he defiantly told the authorities that hanging him would not make a blind bit of difference to their highwayman problem. In this at least, he was telling the truth.

The Bush Inn, St Hilary

There's a lot of folklore about caves and hideaways and secret passageways in and around pubs. Normally, once you scratch the surface, there is no evidence behind them. But Ianto's cave is a real place. The green hilltop west of St Hilary is pitted with shafts and caves opened up long before the Industrial Revolution – early mines that are claimed to have yielded lead and galena up until the eighteenth century, supposedly even some silver, though I cannot swear on the latter.

To this day, Ianto's ghost is a regular sight in the Bush Inn. He is seen with his face contorted in panic, running as fast as he can from one door to another across the main bar area.

BARRY,
THE HOLY DAY
RESORT

Barry is synonymous with the twentieth-century family holiday. Butlins Holiday Camp, Miners' Fortnight, toffee apples, candy floss, bombing in the lido and feeling sick on the rides… Halcyon days.

But Barry has been a holiday destination for a lot longer than you might think.

People have been uncovering Roman artifacts in the Knap area of Barry for some time. Back in 1926, when the lido was being built, ceramic tiles from the era were discovered there. But in the 1980s, when the remains of a Romano-Celtic building were discovered above what is now the Knap car park, no one was altogether sure what it was. But one thing *was* for sure: it had clearly once been quite an imposing structure.

In the vicinity were further ceramic roof tiles, unusual for the time. Meanwhile, chippings dotted around the place suggested that the outside walls would have been clad in dressed or engraved stone – very high end for period.

Still, for all these quirks, at first the consensus was that this was just another Roman villa. In the preceding years, a glut of villas had been found in the Vale, and here it seemed was the annual find, bang on schedule.

But as the details piled up, the picture became less clear. The site's location on the edge of what at the time would have been a water inlet and natural harbour, along the estuary of the Cold Knap, led to speculation that this building might have been part of a port, maybe even a naval outpost.

Some local historians became very excited at this, linking the site to one of the most significant moments in third-century British history.

Around 293, a high-ranking officer in the Roman Army, Marcus Aurelius Mausaeus Carausius, broke with the empire and created his own independent state in Britain. Legend had it that he kept a fleet of 100 war ships, known as the *Classis Britannica*, moored in a harbour somewhere on the South Wales coast. Could that harbour be what had been found in Barry?

Sadly, the odds are against it. The main clue as to the building's purpose is most likely to be the pottery and kitchen-ware uncovered at the site. They would be more in line with commercial use, rather than domestic, let alone military. Most likely, this was Barry's first hotel or B&B, built at the turn of the third and fourth centuries.

However, before you start imaging our Roman forebears relaxing in their togas, carrying their *situlis* and *lingones* and wearing hats with '*da mihi osculum velox*' written across them,* there's another mystery to reckon with. None of the artefacts showed any signs of having ever been used. It seems that the structure never became operational. This being South Wales, perhaps it opened to a particularly miserable summer?

It did at least make one lasting impact on the town, with a lot of its stone being re-used to build Barry Castle.

The remains of Barry's premier Roman resort

There are many other early examples of people heading to Barry for a break.

The monks from the Clas, the monastery at Llancarfan, used Barry Island as a hermitage retreat. One of the island's most famous residents in that respect was St Baruc – so famous, in fact, that Barry is named after him. Baruc was a sixth-century Irish monk, and the legend goes that, while on a retreat at Barry Island, he decided he urgently needed a book, which he knew to be in the library of the monastery on Steep Holm Island, just off the coast.

He rowed out to collect the book but on his return journey got caught in a storm. He battled against the raging sea and howling winds for as long as he could, but in the end he was overpowered by the elements and his boat capsized. His body was discovered washed up on the beach at Jackson Bay and buried on the head-land above, where he had been living in a cave.

Some time later, some fishermen were fishing off Barry Island. They were delighted when they pulled in their nets to find a huge, plump salmon thrashing around in their haul. Heaving it on board their boat, they cut it open to gut it, and what, to their amazement, do you think they found? The book that had cost Baruc his life, in perfect condition.

The book was re-united with the dead monk in his tomb, and shortly after a miracle occurred. The water from the well on the island, which had sustained Baruc in life, suddenly acquired incredible healing powers. As news of this spread, pilgrims travelled from all over the country to visit Barry Island and take the waters, to be cured of injury and ailments.

This pilgrimage became so popular that a chapel had to be built on the site to maintain the shrine and cater for all its visitors. The remains of the chapel are still visible to this day on Friar's Road.

Centuries later, in 1538, John Leyland described Barry Island as follows: 'There ys no dwelling in the isle, but ther is in the midle of it a fair litle chapel of S. Barrok, wher much pilgrimage was used'. So we can surmise that Barry Island remained a place of pilgrimage from the sixth century, right up until the dissolution of the monasteries in the sixteenth century, a thousand years later.

In other words, Barry Island being a 'Holy Day' destination is far from a recent thing. I'll get my coat.

* 'situlis' – Latin for 'buckets'
'lingones' – Latin for 'spades'
'da mihi osculum velox' – Very poor Latin for 'Kiss me quick'

THE MYSTERY OF PORTHKERRY CASTLE

If you have read *The Da Vinci Code*, you will know that the premise of the book hinges on an alleged misspelling in an ancient religious manuscript. Instead of the spelling '*sang real*', meaning royal blood, '*san greal* is written, meaning holy grail.

Over the centuries, ancient scribes have caused no end of debate, all for the want of a good proofreader. And here in Porthkerry, between Barry and Rhoose, we have a most perplexing mystery with a similar problem at its heart.

In the Tudor period, this area was something of a backwater. But it did boast one significant visitor: the esteemed cartographer John Speed, who published a map of the county in 1610. For centuries since, one site marked on this map has perplexed locals and historians and alike: a castle situated in Porthkerry, where no trace of such a castle remains.

What is that all about? Was there ever a castle there? If so, what happened to it? And if not, what was Speed thinking of?

One theory is that there was once a castle in this spot, but that it fell foul of a widely reported natural disaster over 400 years ago. In 1607 a tsunami swept up the Bristol Channel. It became known as the Great Flood, and it devastated vast areas on the coastlines of Somerset, Gloucestershire, Monmouthshire and Glamorgan. There is evidence of this event to be seen to this day, if you know where to look. For example, at the church in the village of Redwick, in south Monmouthshire, an engraving on the outer wall marks the depth of the flood waters. The church also houses a replica of a seventeenth-century wood carving that depicts the carnage of the flood, showing people taking refuge on the roofs of their houses while helpless livestock swim past.

Closer to home there is another relic of the flood, one which you may have seen a hundred times and never registered. In central Cardiff, on the east-facing wall of the Prince of Wales theatre in Wood Street (these days a Wetherspoons pub) you can see the outline in the brickwork of what was once St Mary's Church, which was destroyed by the flood waters. The church may have been destroyed over 400 years ago, but the street on which it once stood still bears its name: St Mary Street.

There are a few pointers to support the theory that Porthkerry Castle was another victim of the flood. For example, St Mary's Church, Cardiff, is also marked on Speed's map, suggesting that, while his map was published in 1610, he must have researched it before the floods of 1607. Moreover, just off the coastline where the castle is marked (near the beach in what is now Porthkerry Country Park), there is a large rock, only visible at low tide, which is known locally as Castle Rock. As the cliffs in this area frequently suffer from rock falls, there is no doubt that this rock was once part of the headland cliffs. Something as powerful as a tsunami would certainly have been capable of ripping such a rock away, whether it had a castle on top of it or not.

The Porthkerry coastline today

For balance, however, we need to look at other, less exciting but altogether more probable explanations.

The case against there having ever been a castle on this site is led by the testimony of a contemporary source: the poet, chronicler and traveller John Leland. As we mentioned in a previous chapter, Leland passed through the area recording his findings in 1538. He made meticulous note of ruins such as Barry Castle, as well as those nearby buildings that were still intact, but his record of the estuary of the Cwm Ciddy in Porthkerry reads, 'There are no notable buildings in the area'.

So what are we to believe? That Speed made a mistake? Made it up? After all, we all have the odd off day.

It is more likely, as my preamble to this chapter might have given away, that this whole episode is just a misinterpretation of language. One thing we know for sure is that there was once an Iron Age hillfort in Porthkerry, possibly dating back to 200 years BC. It is known as the Bulwark, and some of its earthworks and defences are still visible to this day in the woods that surround the site, both as you climb the coastal footpath from Porthkerry Park, and as you approach from the caravan park. Back in the seventeenth century, people were altogether less precise about the distinction between a castle and a fort; the words were interchangeable. I think it is thus very likely that all Speed intended was to mark the Bulwark on his map. Instead, due to the vagaries of language, he managed to spark a debate that has lasted to the modern day.

TOUGH JUSTICE

With characters like the notorious mass murderer Cap Coch lurking in our history, it should come as no surprise that many dark deeds were committed in the Vale of Glamorgan. But sometimes it is difficult to separate the fact from the fiction. Many stories are bathed in the murky waters of hearsay, legend and folklore. For example, the story of the white lady who haunts the Old Place in Llantwit Major, who is said to be the ghost of a woman whose husband starved her to death there. Great murder story, but there is nothing much in the way of evidence to back it up.

So for this chapter, I have delved into the world of the Glamorgan Plea Rolls, the official records kept by the Court of Great Sessions from 1542, hoping to find verifiable evidence of the darker side of our shared history.

Some of the records I found there are every bit as weird and twisted as the accounts passed on to us through the ramblings of the bards. Are you sitting comfortably?

In 1566 the court heard how Lawrence Wick, a labourer from Somerset, murdered Katherine David of St Nicholas on the stroke of midnight on the night of 30th March 1566. He killed her by beating her about the head 'with a hook of the value of two pence', inflicting 'a mortal wound of which she incontinently died'. Then he and an accomplice by the name of David Jevan Dyo set fire to her body and her house to try and cover it all up.

The conclusion of the court was that Dyo should be hung, but there is no record of any punishment being put the way of Wick. So while the accomplice copped it, the murderer appears to have got away scot-free. This is strange to say the least, but nowhere near the weirdest thing about this record.

Firstly, why do we need to know that the hook used to murder poor Katherine was only worth two pence? Would the crime have been taken more seriously if the murderer had used something more expensive? Secondly the word 'incontinently', used to describe how Katherine died: the word means 'without reasonable restraint'. Is the judge saying that Katherine should have made more of an effort to stay alive?

My first question is a little easier to answer than the second. Putting a monetary value on a murder weapon dates to early Anglo-Saxon times, when after a murder trial it was traditional to sell the murder weapon (referred to as a 'deodand') so that it might raise some money to be put to a good cause. That way, at least some good might come of the act. As for Katherine's apparently unconvincing attempts to stay alive upon being beaten across the head with a billhook – we will never know.

Often, the punishments meted out by the establishment of the day were every bit as grisly as the crime themselves. Traditionally men were hung for murder and women were drowned. To modern sensibilities, both methods might seem gruesome enough, but sometimes justices felt a little more creativity was required.

For example, on the 5th of February 1574, the court heard how David ap Hopkyn strangled his wife, Matilda, with a towel in their Cardiff home. A heinous crime, I am sure you will agree, but what really wound up the judge was that the defendant refused to speak a word throughout his trial. It pushed him to such a pique that, in passing sentence, he said (and I quote):

> 'David ap Hopkyn is to be put naked on the ground except his breeches and a hole made under his head and his head put into it and as much stone and iron put upon his body as it will carry and more and he is to be fed on bread and water of the worst kind, bread one day and water another, so kept alive until he dies.'

Harsh.

Given his name, there is every possibility that the defendant David ap Hopkyn only spoke Welsh, and as such didn't offer a defence as he didn't understand the proceedings. In the sixteenth century, the Vale was divided in the languages of its common people. For example, the townsfolk of Cowbridge spoke English, but the traders in the market stalls, who would travel in from the surrounding villages, all spoke Welsh. Despite this, in 1536 Henry VIII decreed that the only languages permissible in Welsh courts were Latin and English. If ap Hopkyn spoke neither, then he probably spent the entire trial trying to figure out what was going on. Whether or not he understood the fate that would befall him, once his sentence was decreed, we will never know. Not to mention whether he would have offered a credible defence, or even offered an alibi, had he understood the discussions going on around him.

In the Tudor period, the crime that had all the male judges and magistrates quivering in their boots was of a wife ridding herself of an unwanted husband by poisoning him. This was considered so serious that it was not classified simply as murder but petty treason. In 1564, Gwenllian Morgan of Cowbridge and Johanna Thomas of Eglwysbrewis were found guilty of killing Gwenllian's husband, Maurice Dee, by feeding him 'ratsbane' concealed in a pudding. In passing sentence, the judge instructed that that they should 'be burned to ashes'.

In this period the principal court of the county was situated in the old town hall in Cardiff, which used to stand in the middle of High Street, near where the entrances to the Castle Arcade and High Street Arcade are today. The county gaol was situated where Cardiff's Indoor Market now stands. But where were the town gallows?

Well, if you have ever referred to the road junction at the top of City Road, Crwys Road, Albany Road and Macintosh Place as 'Death Junction', you may be interested to learn that its nickname doesn't stem from its frequent gridlock, but instead dates all the way back to the sixteenth century, when it became the site of the town's gallows. Its real name was Plwcca Lane, and technically it was not even part of Cardiff back then. It was a very rural area surrounded by farmland.

A blue plaque on the outside wall of the Natwest Bank commemorates the execution of two Catholic priests on this site, Phillip Evans and John Lloyd in 1679. They were convicted of conspiring to assassinate King Charles II, in a case that was something of a stitch up. Both men were made saints in 1970.

How Cardiff's death junction really earned its name

Cardiff, like all major towns and cities at that time, observed something of a tradition when it came to the last passage of a condemned man. And it has led to some interesting linguistic hangovers still in use today.

Hangings were held in public. The idea might turn our stomachs now, but from the fifteenth to the eighteenth century these events were seen as good clean family entertainment, and vast crowds used to turn out to watch them, both at the gallows themselves and along the route that the condemned man travelled to get there.

To spare the condemned man the worst of the pain he was about to endure, it was traditional for his cortege to take an indirect route from Cardiff Gaol to Plwcca Lane, and to stop at every single pub in the city along the way. The procession would pull up outside the first pub and head inside for a few drinks, before climbing back on and heading on to the next one. It's from this practise that we get the expression 'having one for the road'. The only people within the party who wouldn't indulge themselves were the two who still had a job to do: the chaplain and the executioner. They had to stay outside and wait while everyone else indulged.

If you've ever offered to buy someone an alcoholic drink, and they've replied, 'Not for me, thanks, I'm on the wagon,' they are referencing these two abstaining souls and this grisly tradition. Similarly, a reformed alcoholic saying, 'I've fallen off the wagon', meaning they have been abstaining from drink but recently have succumbed to temptation.

And these are not the only expressions this drunkards' procession has contributed to our language today. The stop-start progress of the wagon earned it the nickname 'the lurch', referencing the motion of the horses lunging into action every time they set off, and the sudden stop hurling its passengers forward every time they stopped outside a new pub. If you have ever used the expression 'left in the lurch' to mean being excluded, you are once again referencing the chaplain and the executioner, who had to remain in the cart while everyone else went into the pub.

There are even suggestions that the term 'pub crawl' derives from the pace of this wagon as it progressed towards its ultimate destination, but that remains a matter of speculation.

THE HANGED MAN'S
PILGRIMAGE

In medieval Europe, going on a pilgrimage was an essential part of life. Visiting some site of holy significance, such as the tomb of a saint, was something everyone had to do; as we explored in an earlier chapter, even the king was not excused.

Sometimes the route taken by these pilgrims became every bit as well known as the destination. For example, there is a very famous route called Via Francigena, which starts in Canterbury, England, and winds its way through France and the Swiss Alps to Rome. Another is The Way of St James, a network of paths all over Europe, which converge on Santiago di Compostela in northern Spain.

We have one such route passing through the Bridgend and Vale area, beginning in Swansea and ending in Hereford. It is known as both St Thomas's Way and the Hanged Man Pilgrimage. It was not by any means the most direct route between its start and end points, and it involved crossing the Ewenny River by skipping between the stepping stones at Ogmore Castle, something I am sure many readers of this book will have attempted in the past, and which some will have found, to hilarious effect, not always as easy as it looks. The pilgrimage route then follows the river north and stops at Ewenny Priory, where it crosses the river again, then passes through the town of Bridgend and onto the monastery at Llancarfan, where it re-joins the principal highway of its day and heads east towards St Fagans and Cardiff.

This was a pilgrimage made famous throughout the world by the first people to make it. Under normal circumstances they would have been sworn enemies, but as we shall learn, they were bound together for the most spectacular of reasons. The two people concerned were Lady Mary de Briouze, wife of the Norman lord of Gower; and a commoner and Welsh freedom fighter called William Cragh, who had been found guilty of slaughtering Normans.

The story begins way back in 1283, with a Welsh nobleman called Rhys Ap Maredudd, lord of Ystrad Tywi. He was an ally of the English Crown and had assisted King Edward I in crushing the remaining Welsh strongholds in the old kingdom of Deheubarth, which brought the entire region under Norman control. Sometime after the event, however, around 1290, Rhys felt slighted by the rather paltry rewards he had received in return for his support, so changed sides and mounted his own rebellion. It was short-lived. By 1292 he had been captured, arrested, and executed.

During the height of his brief revolt, however, he had under his command a warrior from Llanrhidian (on the north Gower coast), and this was William Cragh. Cragh and a detachment of men had mounted a raid on one of the castles of William de Briouze, the Norman lord of Gower. The fighting was intense, but when it was concluded, Cragh and fourteen others had been captured by de Briouze's son. There had been a lot of Norman bloodshed in the attack, and for his part, Cragh stood charged with the murder of thirteen men.

There are conflicting reports of what sort of a man Cragh was. In some records he is described as having been nothing more than a common thief and a man of low social standing. For context, however, it is worth pointing out that these records were kept by the Norman authorities. They had good reason to vilify a rebel who had slaughtered them in their droves.

There is strong counterevidence to suggest that Cragh was in fact a man of means, or at the very least, a man with a lot of influence. In the Wales of the thirteenth century, it was possible for a convicted criminal to dodge true justice by paying compensation to the victims of their crimes. In Cragh's case, the 'victim' was the lord of Gower, who suddenly found himself with thirteen positions to fill. Cold comfort for the families of those men.

Cragh's family offered de Briouze 100 head of cattle for his release. This would have been seen as a massive offer, certainly not within the means of a common petty thief. However de Briouze refused the offer, feeling that Cragh needed to be seen to face Norman justice. That de Briouze was willing to forego such a payment, in favour of setting an example, suggests that he knew his actions would be noted – in other words, that Cragh was a sufficiently influential figure amongst the Welsh for them to take note of the proceedings.

This is a point further emphasised by de Briouze's release of twelve of the other men captured alongside Cragh. William Cragh and Trahaern ap Hywel (who was descended from a Welsh nobleman) were the only two who stood trial. Throughout his trial, Cragh pleaded his own innocence. However, both men were found guilty and sentenced to be hung. They were imprisoned in de Briouze's castle in Swansea to await execution.

The appointed day came, and Cragh and ap Hywel were led out onto the town square, in front of the castle in Swansea, to face the gallows. The hanging of Trahaern ap Hywel went without incident, but when Cragh's turn came, the scaffold collapsed, and he was dragged back into prison.

You must bear in mind that, back then, people were far more superstitious and God-fearing than today. To them, the confounding of the planned execution was a potent sign of God's will being that Cragh should not die. There were many ancient laws, in many parts of the world, that stipulated that if a condemned person was spared by an act of nature or God, then the prisoner should be allowed to go free.

De Briouze, however, had other ideas. For him, Cragh had to swing from the gallows. These Welsh rebels needed to be shown their place. He had a new scaffold built and a new date was set for Cragh's execution. Many people were uncomfortable with the decision, including, it would seem, his own wife, Lady Mary de Briouze.

When Cragh was again taken into the town square to be hung, this time the scaffold held strong. There seemed little doubt that the execution had gone ahead without a hitch.

At least at first.

There are quite long and detailed accounts of the hanging and its aftermath: Cragh's body hung there for several days, his head bloated with blood that could not circulate past the noose. I'll spare you the rest of the gory details, but suffice it to say that, when he was cut down from the gallows, Cragh was unquestionably dead.

Which makes everything that happened next very odd indeed. In later years, when questioned, Lady Mary de Briouze could never give a satisfactory answer as to why she had interceded on Cragh's behalf. But intercede she did, praying to a former bishop of Hereford, Thomas de Cantilupe, asking that Cragh be brought back to life.

It's not as if de Briouze and Cragh were friends. They were on opposing sides of a very messy and unpleasant war, and Cragh had been caught raiding one of her castles and slaughtering her guards. Lady de Briouze had had no previous dealings with Cragh. It's all a bit of a mystery.

And that's just the start of it. Everything about Lady Mary's actions is strange, right down to her choice of intercessor.

Even if you are prepared to believe that it is possible to bring people back to life (and believe me, I am just going to skirt around that one), Thomas de Cantilupe was not exactly an obvious person to pray to. He was not at the time a saint, nor had he ever been associated with miracles during his lifetime. He had died several years earlier after a noneventful life as a bishop. However you look at it, he was a very strange choice. But strange or not, the *really* odd thing is… It worked! Cragh did indeed come back to life, days after several witnesses had pronounced him dead.

Now I know what you're thinking. There are countless accounts of dodgy miracles from the mediaeval period. This is just another one of those, right?

While it is true that in this period there are lots of similar stories, from across Europe, most of them do not come with much in the way of corroborating evidence. But in this instance we have a boatload of recorded testimony, witness statements, even cross examination by inquisitors.

I will leave it up to you to decide which parts of the story to believe or disbelieve, but on the basis of reliable historical record, it seems more likely than not that somehow Cragh lived for another eighteen years after he had been officially pronounced dead.

The reason there is so much contemporary record about this case is that the story spread around much of the known world. It put Swansea on the map. When Pope John XXII got to hear about it, he was a bit sceptical. He summoned all the major players (excluding Cantelupe, of course), including the executioner, the guards, the chaplain who had read the last rights, Lady Mary de Brouize, William Cragh, and the men who had cut him down from the gallows, to meet him for an audience in Rome.

They were all rigorously questioned by a panel who recorded every word that was said. By the end of the process, the Pope was so convinced of the details of the stories that in 1320 he canonised Thomas de Cantilupe and posthumously made him a saint, proclaiming the resurrection of William Cragh to be a bonafide miracle.

Now, assuming that we all accept this miracle verdict, I am sure that there is still one other detail that must be bothering you. If you have been paying attention in previous chapters (and books), you may well be questioning the route chosen by Lady Mary and the revenant Cragh for their subsequent pilgrimage.

If someone in fourteenth-century Wales wanted to travel from Swansea to Hereford, there were already two tried and tested routes for them to take, both far more direct than this one. Either the Ridgeway over the uplands of Margam,

Llangeinor and Llantrisant (as taken by William the Conqueror), or the Via Julia Maritima, the Roman road that ran directly between Neath and Gloucester. These would have been far more conventional routes for the pilgrims to follow. But instead, this unlikely party chose to meander through Tythegston, Candleston, Merthyr Mawr and Ogmore Village.

My theory is that this route allowed them to visit and pay homage to the ancestors and descendants of the newly canonised Saint Thomas de Cantilupe.

Ogmore Castle today

According to the Despenser survey of 1320 (named after the Marcher lord of Glamorgan Hugh Depsenser), a man called Robert de Cantelupe was recording as residing in the Tythegston area. He is believed to have built Candleston Castle, which now stands on the edge of the sand dunes near Merthyr

Mawr. Back then this was all good arable farmland; the sands would not arrive for another 200 years. (Incidentally, the name Candleston is believed to be a corruption of 'de Cantelupe's Town', indicating that the family were significant players in the area.)

Records also show that a Mabel de Cantelupe, likely to be the saint's sister, or at least a cousin, had lived locally too. It is possible (though there is little concrete proof) that she had been married to Maurice de Londres, who you will of course remember from an earlier chapter as both the lord of Ogmore Castle and also the benefactor of Ewenny Priory. She died in Bridgend in 1267.

The person we believe to have been her granddaughter, Hawise de Chaworth (née de Londres), lived in Ogmore Castle with her husband Patrick at the time of this pilgrimage. In fact, that same year she had inherited the lordships of Ogmore and Kidwelly, upon the death of her brother William. His tomb can still be seen in the church at Ewenny Priory. 1320 was an eventful year for the de Cantelupes and their descendants, to say the least.

Granted, there is a fair amount of conjecture to my theory, but it does at least start to explain why a route from Swansea to Hereford might involve crossing at the stepping stones by Ogmore Castle, and also why a visit to Ewenny Priory and Bridgend should have been on the cards.

The contemporary fame of this story reached far and wide, and made Cragh and de Brouize superstars of their era. As they progressed along their pilgrimage, crowds would turn out to cheer them on their way. Cragh clearly was something of a showman, as records say that he made the entire pilgrimage with a noose hanging from around his neck. Thankfully, the monks they visited along the way were very thorough in recording their visits, describing exactly where they went, what they said, even what they ate and drank. If Instagram had existed in the fourteenth century, they would have been plastered all over it.

#bestlife #2ndlife.

THE FIRST WAVE OF
COOL CYMRU

I mentioned in my chapter about the Tubervilles that, for a brief period towards the end of the nineteenth and the beginning of the twentieth centuries, Welshness, and in particular Welsh gothic fantasy stories, became very fashionable. Cool Cymru was the order of the day.

This movement was pioneered by two eccentric characters from Glamorgan: Dr William Price and Edward Williams, better known as Iolo Morgannwg. Both of them were very well educated, very intense and very intelligent men, both very patriotic and nationalistic, and both fascinated with the druids and pagan Celtic worship. And both enjoyed a certain degree of celebrity and notoriety in their day.

Edward Williams was born near Flemingston, a small village in the Vale of Glamorgan, in 1747. His father was a stone mason, a very sought-after trade at the time. Edward Williams himself tried his hand at the profession, but like so many things, he never really took to it.

Even from his early days he took an interest in Welsh history and poetry and was an avid collector of ancient manuscripts. His talent, though, was romanticising. As a poet and a writer, his works were full of passion, and his true love was undoubtedly Wales and Welsh culture.

He moved to London in 1773 and cut a dashing figure about the town. His charm and charisma made him the darling of all the London-Welsh literary societies. He had a theory (which still has quite a following today) that ancient druidic tradition survived long after the Romans introduced Christianity – that, in fact, Arthurian Welsh culture flourished in the dark ages, growing increasingly distinct in its religion and rich in its literature, until it was eventually destroyed by the invading English.

Five years later he returned to Wales, took a wife and had a son (who he named Talisien after the twelfth-century bard). He also tried his hands at farming (unsuccessfully). He first came to prominence in 1789, when he published *Barddoniaeth Dafydd ab Gwilym*, under the name of Iolo Morgannwg. This was a collection of poems by the fourteenth-century Welsh poet Dafydd ap Gwilym. In this book he published many hitherto unknown works which he claimed to have re-discovered.

Alongside his literary efforts, Williams was a prolific antiquarian and published many works piecing together a revisionist version of Welsh history, literature and culture. His research drew upon his collection of ancient manuscripts, and when the ancient works of *The Mabinogion* and *The Book of Tailesen* were re-discovered, it was Williams' pioneering work that allowed experts to translate them for modern consumption.

Williams is also famous for having rekindled the ancient and secret order known as the Gorsedd of the Bards, and along with it the institution of the Eisteddfod. He developed a runic system known as the bardic alphabet, and he was retained as a bard by the Wyndham-Quinn family, the earls of Dunraven Castle. He is also regarded as an anti-slavery campaigner, proudly hanging outside his shop in Cowbridge a sign declaring that all the sugar sold inside had been produced on plantations worked only by free men. However, when his brother died, Edward Williams fiercely contested his exclusion from the will, the fortune in question having been entirely amassed from plantations that did employ slaves.

Sadly, this is indicative of the slender grip on reality that would become Williams' undoing.

At the end of the nineteenth century, Sir John Morris-Jones established that Williams had forged many of the documents he had produced to 'source' his theories. Even former disciples of his work were outraged, feeling betrayed. Williams ended up serving a prison stretch, and the extent of his deceptions were such that, even today, some of his forgeries are better known to the academic community than the genuine documents they replaced.

After the First World War, a scholar called Griffith John Williams was charged with going back through all of Iolo's output, to distinguish what was real and what was not. He declared that it was a crying shame that he had managed to blight his entire output with the deceptions he had pulled, claiming much of it was spot on but acknowledging that now it would never be regarded as such.

Dr William Price was a doctor of medicine born to a working class family in Rudry in 1800. His political beliefs were altogether more authentic than Iolo Morgannwg's, and he was known to be an avid supporter of the Chartists. After the Chartists' march in Newport ended in massacre, he eloped to

France to avoid prosecution for his part in the movement. While he was exiled, he had something of a vision, fuelling a belief that he was the subject of an ancient prophecy, which predicted he would return to Wales to free the nation from English rule.

When he returned to Wales, he adopted a lot of the ideas put forward by Iolo Morgannwg, advocating a neo-druidic movement that he believed had flourished in Wales until its suppression under English rule. He was a charismatic figure, and was successful in recruiting likeminded followers. His beliefs first came to wider attention when, in 1884, after the death of his son, Price cremated his body, something that was unheard of at the time. He was arrested, and his trial was followed intently in newspapers right the way around the world. He successfully argued that his actions were not against the law, paving the way for the Cremation Act to be passed in 1902.

Having so eloquently and publicly defended his right to observe ancient Welsh customs, Price became a national obsession. His timing couldn't have been better: there was, as I said at the beginning of this chapter, a huge appetite in Wales to reconnect with a historical identity long suppressed, as well as a huge appetite in the wider United Kingdom for all things Welsh. In hindsight, this was an opportunity for a true cultural renaissance, and one that was largely squandered.

Price began to engage in activities which earned him the reputation of something of a weirdo. One particular incident that jumps to mind is a letter he sent to *The Daily Telegraph* claiming that all the books of ancient Greece were originally written in Welsh by Welsh bards, that Homer was in fact from Van, near Caerphilly – oh, and that the great poet had also built Caerphilly Castle.

The authority for all this was the writings of the ancient Chinese.

Whatever the veracity of his claims, Price must have done something right. He lived to be ninety-two, eventually dying in Llantrisant. His remains were, as you would expect, cremated, and in front of no less than 20,000 onlookers.

Dr Price's statue overlooking Llantrisant town centre

Both these men were complex characters, probably too complex for me to do them, their beliefs, lives and output justice in this short chapter. Both of them possessed a nationalistic intensity and a desire to rediscover and reinvigorate a culture and identity which we have undoubtedly lost in Wales. But both of them allowed their passion to drive them to clutch at straws and make wild and unsubstantiated claims, and in doing so, undid a lot of the good work they had started.

But whatever you personally may think about their beliefs, about the arguments they put forward, or the theories and conclusions they drew, one thing is for certain: they were never boring.

KING ARTHUR'S
LANDMARK VICTORY

There is a growing tide of opinion, especially in Wales, that stories about King Arthur of Camelot deserve to be taken more seriously as historical accounts. There is no question that these stories have been embellished to include beasts, magic and wizards, but as with all folklore, at their core, there is probably some genuine material which warrants closer examination.

One such story is of a famous battle where the ancient Britons, led by King Arthur, thwarted the invading armies of Saxony, either in the late fifth or early sixth century. The battle was first reported by the esteemed sixth-century monk and historian Gildas, in his work *De Excidio et Conquestu Britanniae* (*On the Ruin and Conquest of Britain*).

Gildas' account tells of the struggles between the ancient Britons and the Germanic hordes of the Angles and the Saxons, who were determined to secure a colony on our shores. His account describes their invasion as a long and hard-fought, piecemeal affair, much like the Norman incursions into South Wales. Gains would be made by one army, then just as quickly overturned. All would go quiet for a while, the Britons daring to hope that the Angles and Saxons had gone home, only for the invaders to return and try again. But at long last, all of that toing and froing came to something of a climax at Badon Hill. This was a decisive victory for the Celtic ancient Britons, inaugurating a period of peace that lasted seventy years

It would seem that the western side of Britain was the hardest part of the country for the invaders to subdue. Hence us being called the 'Welsh' – it's the Saxon word for foreigner. (The nerve!) Modern interpretations of the boundaries between England and Wales would have meant nothing back then. To a Saxon, you might be from Carlisle, Liverpool, Gloucester or Bath, but you were all Welsh to them. As Gildas wrote:

> From that time, the citizens were sometimes victorious, sometimes the enemy, in order that the Lord, according to His wont, might try in this nation of Israel of today, whether it loves Him or not. This continued up to the year of the siege of Badon Hill (*obsessionis Badonici montis*), and of almost the last great slaughter inflicted upon the rascally crew. And this commences, a fact I know, as the forty-fourth year, with one month now elapsed; it is also the year of my birth

Now, to be fair, Gildas' account of the battle does not mention Arthur at all. It has been speculated that the monk had a bit of a beef with Arthur on account of the legendary king having killed his brother. Then again, 200 years later, the venerable Bede (another great monk and historian) gave us his account of this battle, again without mentioning Arthur. In fact, it was another 100 years again before any English chronicles were to cast him in the lead role, the ninth-century scroll *Historia Brittonum* stating, 'battle was on Mount Badon in which there fell in one day 960 men from one charge by Arthur'.

Welsh monks were convinced of his presence, however. The early history of Wales, Annales Cambriae (probably seventh or eighth century but we do not know for sure) describes the battle as follows: 'Arthur carried the Cross of Our Lord Jesus Christ on his shoulders for three days and three nights, and the British were victorious'.

'All very interesting,' you might say, 'but why are you writing about this in a book about the legends of Glamorgan? Badon Hill doesn't exactly sound Welsh.'

Truth be told, nobody knows where Badon Hill is. As I hope the above paragraphs demonstrate, history from this period is sketchy to say the least. Date lines are difficult to match, and place names that have fallen out of use can often suggest any one of a dozen possible locations.One thing we do know, however, is that there is no shortage of reported links between southern Wales and King Arthur.

And as no one is altogether sure either where or when this battle took place, no one should be especially surprised by the theory that it was fought somewhere between Bridgend and Maesteg.

The most extensive account of the exploits of King Arthur and this conflict come from the twelfth-century monk Geoffrey of Monmouth, in his work *Historia Regum Brittaniae*. He was convinced that the site of Camelot was Caerleon, near Newport, and thought that Badon was the city of Bath. Quite a few historians disagree, arguing that the hamlet of Badebury in Wiltshire is a more likely candidate. It sort of makes sense: Badebury does at least sounds a bit like Badon, and it also lies on an ancient roadway that was in use at the time. In fact, it is on the same route as the Ridgeway, along the English stretch that terminates in London.

King Arthur approaching Camelot, as depicted at the height of the nineteenth-century Celtic revival

However, if we're talking linguistic closeness, plus proximity to the seat of Arthur's power, anyone with an Ordinance Survey map can verify that above Coytrahen, between

Bridgend and Maesteg, is a hill called Mynydd Baeden. Some very enthusiastic local historians will tell you that this is the true site of Badon. And it is not an absurd suggestion.

Just like Badebury, the name sounds about right. Also like Badebury, it is on a stretch of the Ridgeway, at a point where the route intersects with another ancient road called Ffordd y Gyfraith, which runs north from Laleston to Llangynwyd. So while this is a quiet spot today, back in the fifth century, it would have been a prime spot to drive an army to. Not only that, but any fifth-century strategist would have recognised its value, as is evidenced by the Bronze and Iron Age earthworks scattered all over it. The peak of this hill is a very long and flat plain, with outstanding views: a perfect battlefield, depending on how much of it was covered in trees back then.

But do I have any proof for any of this? Well, there have been archaeological digs on the summit of Mynydd Baeden, and there is evidence of the area having been populated at this point in history. Moreover, a lot of bodies have been discovered, supporting the notion of a battle having taken place there. But more work is needed to establish the true scale of either. In other words, watch this space. I am sure we will hear more about this site in the future.

BALLS AGAINST
THE WALL

If you have ever been to watch a Six Nations international at the Principality Stadium, you will have no illusions about the Welsh passion for sport. This is evident throughout our history. In pre-Tudor years, there was very tight regulation around how much time the peasantry were allowed to spend in any pursuits of this kind, landowners fearing that, without such restrictions, the whole feudal system might just fall apart.

Monday to Saturday were for toil and labour on the land, and Sunday was for church, contemplative prayer and other such activities that were good for the soul.

During the reign of Henry VIII, it was decreed that every man in the kingdom should spend one day a week practising his archery. In Glamorgan, ever since the Battle of Agincourt, we had a reputation for producing the finest bowmen in Europe, so this was especially well observed locally, particularly in the Llantrisant area.

But if archery wasn't your bag, then the only time left for ordinary people to play sport was during festivals and holy days. That is not necessarily as restrictive as it might sound. One of the big plus points of everyone being so dedicated to the Church was the number of holy days throughout the year, as well as the length of festivals like Christmas, which used to run right up until Candlemas (in February).

So, while much of the life of a medieval peasant left a lot to be desired, they did at least get fifty-one days of holiday a year. And this time was spent in all manner of gaming. In fact, this was how most village fairs began, a tradition we still see observed in many places to this day.

The Bull Ring, Llantrisant

Records of folk football, the forerunner to the beautiful game, go back as far as the twelfth century. By the Tudor period, it was played pretty much everywhere in Britain. Entire villages would meet in open ground to play a game that was a halfway house between football and British Bulldog.

Folk football was simple: one team tried to kick an inflated sheep's bladder from one point to another, while their opposition tried to stop them from getting through. Then the opposing team would have a go. These games could get so violent that there are multiple seventeenth-century records of people's cause of death that read 'playing football'.

By the eighteenth century, medieval restrictions on people's use of their time had been relaxed (slightly). Suddenly the Welsh peasantry didn't know what to do with themselves. Well, actually they knew *exactly* what to do with themselves: bando, by now the biggest sport in Glamorgan.

This was a primitive form of hockey, played between parishes in the area. It was usually around twenty a side, although numbers do seem to vary. Like folk football, it was a pretty brutal affair, and games tended to bring out the tribal nature of people. The bando from which the game took its name was a stick made of oak, ash or elm and shaped like a modern hockey stick. The object of the game was to hit the ball – called a colby – into a goal. Beyond that, there did not seem to be any rules at all.

A letter written in 1777, by Rhys Thomas, a printer from Cowbridge, describes 'the countryside between Bridgend and Pyle [being] rendered barren of ash or elm by the heavy use of those woods for the making of bando sticks'.

And it wasn't just Bridgend and Pyle that caught bando fever. In Margam, the game was played three times a week, and thousands would turn out, decked out in ribbons and favours of their team's colours, to watch their idols do battle.

As you would expect from a game with such a passionate following, a great deal of civic pride was attached to the bragging rights of tournament winners. Pyle, Kenfig and Margam were famously great rivals, but according to the writings of Charles Redwood in his work *The Vale of Glamorgan*, published in 1839, it was Llantwit Major who considered themselves a bit above the others. He described their behaviour as 'exceedingly hoity-toity among the neighbouring villages, and [they] carried everything with a high hand'.

Another gaming tradition now disappeared was the gŵyl mabsant, which started out in the Middle Ages as a religious festival. The date of the festival varied from place to place, as it was linked to whichever saint the local parish church was dedicated to. But it always began on the Sunday following the saint's feast day, and usually ran for a week, sometimes two.

By the eighteenth century, the religious significance of the gŵyl mabsant had dwindled, and the festival was dying out, much to the consternation of local inn keepers, who had always done rather well out of it. Reluctant to see it end, they took charge and turned it into an almighty knees-up, with lots of boozing, blood sports and gambling at its heart. And that went down rather well with the eighteenth-century locals.

One of the staples of this event was bull baiting, which basically consisted of releasing a pack of dogs onto a bull. The account books of both the Cardiff Corporation and the township of Llantrisant list 'bull ropes' as town expenditure in 1712, and of course Llantrisant's Bull Ring is so named as it was once the site of such events. The bull terriers of Llantrisant were famous in their day; a letter from Thomas Rees to Cadrawd, dated 12th January 1907, described 'a celebrated breed of white [bull] terriers at Llantrisant'.

Sadly, this was not the only blood sport spectacle at these events. Cockfighting was also a common sight, so much so that we had our own local variant of it, known as Welsh Main. Even with the sensibilities of the time, this was seen by many as barbaric. The Reverend Pegge gives us an account of it, written in 1775:

> It consists of sixteen pairs of cocks; of these sixteen conquerors are pitted a second time; the eight conquerors of these are pitted a third time; the four conquerors a fourth time so that thirty one cocks are sure to be most inhumanly murdered for the sport and pleasure, the noise and nonsense, nay, I may say, the profane cursing and swearing of those who have the effrontery to call themselves... Christians.

Incidentally, his indignation was not necessarily shared elsewhere in the Church. In fact, the flat surface of a tomb in a churchyard was a common arena for this sport, and there are even instances of cockfights taking place inside the churches themselves.

Much like the gallows, these blood sports have left their mark on modern language. The term 'cockpit', for example, is derived from their association with the similarly tight enclosures where birds were 'pitted' against each other. You yourself may have been 'pitted' against someone in your time. Then, having defeated your rival, you could have been said to have 'earned your spurs', harking back to the tradition of champion birds being allowed to wear spurs on their heels as a mauling weapon. Even the expression 'I'm game', meaning

I am up for taking part in something, references how fighting cocks were once known as 'game birds'.

Some gŵyl mabsant became so famous that they would draw people from far and wide. Charles Wesley described the festivals taking place at St Fagans, Dinas Powys, Whitchurch and Michaelstone-Super-Ely as 'revels' and 'riots'. Mr Wesley was famous for many things but he was not exactly a good-time Charley. He was outraged by the goings on he had seen. And when it came to drunken debauchery it seems Whitchurch set the standard:

> 'Tues. September 15th 1741… I was at another famous revel in Whitchurch which lasts a week and is honoured with the presence of the gentry and clergy, far and near. I put myself in their way, and called 'awake thou that sleepest, and arise from the dead, and Christ shall give thee light'. I trust there was a great awakening among the dead souls'.

Cockfighting aside, there has always been an uneasy relationship between sports and the Church in Wales. One sport which really pushed its luck was simply called ball. It was a game similar to fives, resembling if you will squash but without rackets. To play, you needed a fairly wide space and a high stone wall. Back then, that usually meant the outer wall of the village church. You can imagine the priest's displeasure, his attention drawn from a learned manuscript or a needy parishioner by the *thump, thump, thump* of the ball against his walls.

Legislation making this practise illegal was passed in the

sixteenth century. But ball carried on unabated. An account of a Sunday morning in 1820 tells of the Reverend Thomas Roderick, curate of the parish church of Llantrisant, standing at the front of his church, ready to deliver his Sunday service, but affronted to find most of the pews empty. The tell-tale sound of merriment emanating from the churchyard roused his suspicions.

His robes billowing about him, he stormed out of the church and into the churchyard.

'Dewch nawr, fechgin, mae'n amser,' he bellowed, meaning, 'Come now, boys. It is time.'

'Treiwch un pel cyn dechrau'r gwasanaeth,' came the reply, meaning, 'Try one ball before beginning the service.'

Indignant, the reverend slammed the ball against the wall of the church with so much vigour that it bounced off like a bullet, whistling past the ears of the other players and lodging itself in the ground behind a grave. Jaws dropped, and the eyes of the dumbstruck players nearly popped out of their heads. A few minutes later, the church was full of sweaty, muscular men in their shirtsleeves, eager to hear the gospels with a newfound respect.

This spirit of 'if you can't beat them, join them' was also in evidence in Cardiff in 1777, when the custodians of St John's Church became so frustrated with the constant game playing against their north wall that they financed the first recorded example of a public court. This stood roughly where the Owain Glyndŵr pub stands today. The building that preceded this pub was itself known as Tennis Court Hotel. Much to the relief of reverends across the land, by the time this hotel was built, ball had fallen out of favour, and people had forgotten the court's original purpose.

MUSING ON PLACE NAMES IN GLAMORGAN

I ended my first book with a chapter of ramblings about place names in and around Bridgend and the Vale of Glamorgan, and where they probably come from. From subsequent feedback, I was delighted to learn that I am not the only one absorbed by this subject. Some of what follows was supplied to me by people who have done their own research, and who contacted me to share what they have found.

We have so many influences that make up the tapestry of our place names. The church, legends, famous sons, Viking navigators, battles and wars, Roman and English invaders, aristocratic landowners, and Welsh 'matter-of-fact' descriptions. A rather eminent French toponymist (whose name escapes me) once described place names as 'fossils of human geography'. In other words, they are not history in and of themselves, but they are the scars left behind by the movement of history and people.

For example, in the central and inland areas of the Vale of Glamorgan, we have a lot of villages with names ending in 'ton', such as Boverton, Pickerston, Bonvilston, and Gileston; this convention also reaches further west, with Tythegston,

Newton and Laleston. This can also be seen in the names of ancient farms.

The language of the Vale of Glamorgan was not consistent. Up until 1536 (when the Act of Union was passed by Henry VIII, making English the official language of Wales) there were English-speaking pockets and Welsh-speaking pockets. Today, if you want a clue as to where the English bits were, you will not go far wrong simply circling wherever ends in 'ton'. (And make sure to include 'Sutton', which is what the English settlers called Ogwr, now reverted back to Ogmore.

The word 'tun' derived from the Saxon for 'farmstead', 'enclosure' or more latterly 'estate'.

Before the Norman invasion, the Saxons never made much of an impression in Wales beyond Monmouthshire. However, when English settlers arrived in South Wales as part of the twelfth-century Norman invasion, their ranks were made up of many different ethnic influences, people descended from any number of invading or settling factions – including Saxons.

There were also descendants of the same ancient Britons as the Welsh themselves, as well as Angles, Vikings, French and Normans. And bear in mind that the Normans themselves were descended from Vikings who had settled in Northern France. The language of these people would have been an exotic cocktail made up of all of these influences.

To give you an idea of the differences between this language and modern day English, it's worth contrasting a few lines of literature that have been transformed across the ages. This text has been in perpetual use since the twelfth century. For those not familiar with the modern version, these are the opening stanzas of Psalm 23, which is commonly read during funerals:

The LORD is my shepherd, I lack nothing.
He makes me lie down in green pastures, he leads
     me beside quiet waters,
he refreshes my soul.
He guides me along the right paths for his name's
     sake.
Even though I walk through the darkest valley, I
     will fear no evil, for you are with me; your rod
     and your staff, they comfort me.

Back in the medieval period, this exact same passage, written in what is known as Middle English, read as follows:

Lauerd me steres, noght wante sal me:
In stede of fode þare me louked he.
He fed me ouer watre ofe fode,
Mi saule he tornes in to gode.
He led me ouer sties of rightwisenes,
For his name, swa hali es.
For, and ife I ga in mid schadw ofe dede,
For þou wiþ me erte iuel sal I noght drede;

A bit of a difference, I'm sure you'll agree. That's how Saxon words like 'ton' crept into our area, and also how they slipped out again. By the fifteenth century, after the initial influx of settlers was over, you do not find fields, farms and villages with 'ton' in their names, as by this time the word was falling out of common use.

   We do not see another influx of population from outside the area until the seventeenth century, when trading between the booming ports of Aberthaw and Minehead saw many from Somerset and Devon marrying into Vale families and settling here. The same thing happened in reverse, with Vale families settling around Minehead. As a result, field and farm names in this period start to take on nuances specific to Somerset and Devon, rather than more general English.

When trying to decipher the origins of place names, it is important to remember that they change largely through corruptions of language. For example, there is a farm in St Andrews called Greenyard, which may sound innocuous enough. However, with a bit of surface scratching on old title deeds, you discover that in 1566 it was known as Grenet. Between 1785 and 1813, this somehow changed to Greenett, then 1796-1819 it was Greenard. To get to the bottom of it, you need to go back to the sixteenth century, where the same title deeds give the answer. In 1566, the land was bequeathed in the will of one John Grennett: the name of the farm today, Greenyard, is simply a corruption of the name of the Grennett family who once owned it.

Just because we are in Wales, it does not follow that the Welsh name of a place is its original one. Some places did not come into existence until after the English invasion, and were only ever occupied by English settlers. As such, they never had a Welsh name to begin with. However, due to the same trend of corruption described in the last example, over time English mutations often end up sounding like Welsh.

We have a fantastic example in Dinas Powys, where there is a place called Twyncyn. At first glance this might appear to be a natural enough partnering of the Welsh 'Twyn', meaning hill, and the diminutive suffix 'cyn', which qualifies that the hill in question is quite small. The Twyncyn in question being situated on a slight elevation, this all fits together beautifully. Our work here is done. Time for a pint.

But as plausible as all this sounds, you need to bear in mind that Dinas Powys was an English-speaking area. Do a little digging and you discover that, back in 1785, Twyncyn was known as 'Tomkins Land', and a lane leading to it was called 'Tomkins Lane'. So in reality, this otherwise very plausible Welsh name of Twyncyn, 'place on the small hill', is in fact only a Cymruification of the original English Tomkin.

Not all foreign settlers in Glamorgan were invaders of course. There are all sorts of reasons why settlers came to the area. For example, the arrival of Hugenots from France escaping persecution under the reign of Louis XV, and more latterly the draw of mass employment during the industrial revolution. But outside these well-known migrations, we have quite an unusual place name in the area that marks another, lesser known exodus.

It can be found in a secluded valley in Pant, below Heol-y-Mynydd on the edge of Southerndown Golf Club. During the latter part of the fourteenth century, on the other side of Europe in the low countries, an entire way of life was under threat. Flanders had grown very rich on the back of a booming textile industry. Centres of production like Bruges and Ghent would employ as many people as they could find to work in the industry, which led to rapid urbanisation. By 1450 over one third of the population of Flanders lived in these two places alone.

But every boom is followed by a bust, and by the turn of the fifteenth century, the market had collapsed. There was mass unemployment and living conditions in the region's towns and cities became intolerable. Many fled to Britain to escape the recession and to start up textile making over here. One such family ended up in this little valley. We know this as the well situated in the middle of the valley has ever since been known as 'the Marie Flanders Well'.

One local place name that has been the subject of much supposition is the Tumble. This steep hill carries the A48 away from M&S in Culverhouse Cross, out onto the pastures on the plateau of the Vale, around the villages of the Downs, St George and St Nicholas. There is another place called Tumble near Llanelli. Both are on steep hills, and I always assumed that their names were something to do with tumbling down the hill, like Jack and Jill, on account of this steepness.

However, I recently came across the writings of Charles F Shepperd. Back in 1962, he wrote that this hill was originally known as Tumbledown Dick, and that the people of Wenvoe were convinced that its name was a reference to a story from local history. It is well documented that Richard Cromwell, the son and heir of Lord Protector Oliver Cromwell, was very close to Colonel Philip Jones of Fonmon Castle. In fact Jones' hold over Cromwell was so all encompassing that it was once asked in Parliament why it was that England appeared to be being run from 'a small castle in Wales'. One day, after what must have been a very boozy lunch, Richard Cromwell was heading back to London from Fonmon when he had a rather spectacular fall on this steep section of road. And that is what led to it being known as 'Tumble Down Dick'. In 1659, the dismissal of Richard Cromwell led to the restoration of the monarchy, and the end of the rather pious, Puritan-led Commonwealth of England.

But Shepperd had his doubts as to this explanation. Instead, he suggested Norse origins, brought to us by Viking traders who, looking to set up shop outside the city of Cardiff, chose a crossroads on a main road as the logical place to do so. He speculates that these enterprising Vikings described the new home of their business with the Norse word '*Turberns-dune*', meaning 'the down of thunder'. It is this, Shepperd suggests, that is at the bottom of today's 'Tumble'.

For my final place name, I must travel west to Stormy Down (between Pyle and Laleston). I have to confess that, once again, I did not initially think there was much of a story here. I grew up near Stormy Down, and I knew how windy and exposed it was. A down that suffered from storms – what could be simpler? Oh how wrong I was.

In 1150, a Norman noble by the name of Geoffrey Sturmi was made the warden of a boar hunt on Newton Down by the earls of Glamorgan, the De Claires. Sturmi was very well acquainted with hunting; in fact, his personal seal was an effigy of himself with a hunting horn and a boar spear.

He built a motte and bailey castle known as Sturmi's Castle. The first reference to it is from 1154, in a record of a dispute between the parish churches of Kenfig and Newcastle, Bridgend, who both wanted to charge it a tithe. Archbishop Theobald of Canterbury had to settle the dispute, and he did so in favour of the older St Leonard's Church, Newcastle.

The castle was a little isolated, on the turbulent western front of Norman Wales, and it frequently suffered from Welsh raids. Whether it was the crippling cost of fending off these attacks, or for some other reason, the Sturmi family fell on hard times. The last Sturmi to occupy the castle, Roger Sturmi, eventually sold up his castle and lands to Margam Abbey in 1179. The monks turned it into a grange, and a recent aerial photograph has located its position.

This is the perfect example of how a seemingly innocuous name can contain so much history: the rise and fall of a family, on the vanguard of a great invasion. Next time you find yourself driving through the towns, villages and farms of Glamorgan, ponder for a while what their names might tell you about their history.

PART TWO

MYTHS, FOLKLORE AND THE SUPERNATURAL

I WANT TO SUCK
YOUR GWAED

Vampires may not normally be associated with Welsh folklore, but I recently came across a series of articles which amount to vampire stories set in South Wales. They are quite unique when compared to contemporary stories from elsewhere, and there is a very definite theme uniting them.

When you think of more famous vampire stories, like *Dracula* and *Nosferatu*, the monsters are (at least most of the time) visible: characters with personality, back stories and a physical presence. But in the Welsh tradition, vampires are not seen, and little is known about their identities. They are also generally connected to an inanimate object, such as an item of furniture, rather than able to wander wherever they like under the cover of darkness. They also do not appear to be put off by crosses and religious paraphernalia.

But they are, nonetheless, recognisably vampiric. The following tales are fairly typical of the genre and were first published by Marie Trevelyan in 1909.

A large old farmhouse, on the edge of the Brecon Beacons was taken over by new tenants. They discovered that some old furniture belonging to the previous occupants still filled many of the rooms. This was not really a problem, as they did not plan to make general use of these rooms. But when a pious minister was to stay as a weekend guest, the rooms were dusted down, and a fire lit in the hearth.

The minister was to preach at the local chapel that Sunday. He arrived on the Friday night quite exhausted by his journey, and retired to his chamber early. He sat in an armchair by the window and read from his Bible, before falling asleep. Throughout the night he was tormented by bad dreams, and when he woke, he spotted a wound on the back of his hand. It was bleeding. He wrapped it with a handkerchief, and over breakfast commented to the lady of the house that a couple of nails in the armchair might need attention.

She was shocked to hear this. A previous visitor had stayed in the room and complained of the same thing. She had already had the armchair overhauled by an upholsterer. She went to the room and checked the chair over herself, but could find nothing that might have caused the minister's wounds.

The following evening, having once more spent some hours reading his Bible, the minister again fell asleep in the armchair. He was awoken by a feeling 'as if being gnawed at by a dog'. A pain ran down the whole left-hand side of his body. He felt so weak that he struggled to get to his feet and strike a light. When he finally did, he lifted his shirt to find wounds across his rib cage. They were just like those on the back of his hand, and all of them were oozing with blood.

On Sunday morning, as the congregation were leaving the chapel, the minister was introduced to the landlady of the farmhouse. He said to her, 'Madam, you may or may not know it, but I believe a vampire frequents your house. The dead man who owned the furniture comes to suck the blood from intruders and is probably not pleasantly disposed towards ministers of the Gospels.'

To which she replied, 'It has happened to two ministers before you.'

An exorcism was held, and when the minister departed the house, he declared that the malignant spirit had been put to rest. But in 1850, a dignitary of the Church of England came to stay and reported the same unpleasant experience, showing similar wounds on his left hand, arm, and leg.

I'm no expert on these matters, but surely just get rid of the chair?

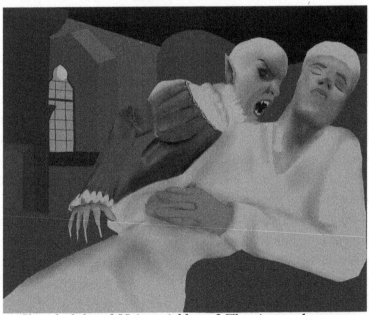

Clean bed sheets? Noisy neighbours? The nineteenth-century traveller had bigger things to worry about...

Similar stories from this era involve other items of furniture. One concerns a Cardiff family who bought a four-poster bed dating from the reign of King James I. It was bought at a bankruptcy auction, where the lot was described as a 'handsome but heavy piece of furniture'. The successful bidder placed it in his best bedroom and was proud to exhibit it to his friends, but it was never used – not until one day when some building work was being carried out in the main bedroom. The man who had bought the bed was away at the time, leaving his wife and their four-month-old baby daughter to spend a few nights in the spare bedroom alone.

The first evening they slept in the bed, the child was very restless, but otherwise the night passed without incident. On the second night, the child suddenly cried out violently, startling her mother, who could not pacify her.

In the morning, the mother sent for the doctor, who examined the infant but could find nothing of concern. So before bedtime, the mother gave the baby a warm bath and sang her gently into a deep sleep. But in the middle of the night, the child let out a terrifying scream. The mother sat bolt upright in the bed and took the babe up in her arms. She spotted a red circular incision in the centre of her babe's neck. It was oozing blood.

She summoned the doctor once again (those were the days!) He examined the child and her injury for a long time, before remarking, 'It is just as though something has caught at the child's throat and sucked the blood as one would suck an egg…'

Countryfolk in rural parts of Glamorgan used to believe that vampires particularly liked to suck on the corpses of the damned. One story tells of an old yeoman, known to be money-grasping and mean. It was often said that he could 'suck blood out of a stone'. I'm pretty sure you can see where this is going.

When he died, he was duly laid out to rest, and his 'death chamber' was shut up for the night. His remaining relatives sat by the fire in vigil, in the next room. During the night, they repeatedly heard scratching noises emanating from the death chamber, but were too frightened to investigate in the dark. In the morning, they found the shroud that had been placed over the body had been disturbed, and the body was covered in puncture marks. The date of the funeral was brought forward a day 'for fear the body would be entirely devoured'.

The moral of the story? If in death you want to rest in peace, and not in pieces, always tip your waiter.

THE QUIRKY FAMILY
OF ST CADOC

No matter how embarrassing your father may have appeared to you when you were growing up, compared to St Cadoc, you had it easy.

As we have touched on in other chapters, St Cadoc was one of the most revered saints of the early Christian church. He was born in the latter quarter of the fifth century, over 1,500 years ago, and we still name schools, churches, hospitals, community centres and streets after him to this day – to say nothing of the village of Cadoxton on the outskirts of Barry.

The life of St Cadoc is recorded in the ancient works of *The Cambro British Saints*. His story contains the first ever reference to the now legendary King Arthur of Camelot. Amongst Cadoc's achievements are the founding of the Clas, a monastery at Llancarfan, near Cowbridge, as well as many churches throughout Wales, Scotland, Ireland, and Brittany. He also managed to find time for the odd miracle – even as a baby. It is claimed that he turned the water of the font in which he was baptised into milk.

All these achievements, however, were in spite of a dysfunctional upbringing that wouldn't look out of place in a Channel 5 documentary.

First of all, he was not the only saint in the family. Pretty well his whole family were saints, including his father. All I can say is, I think the bar for sainthood must have been set pretty low back then, because his father was a brute, a drunkard, and a pirate. Oh yes, and a king. He was called Gwynllyw, although somehow in later history this got Anglicised to Woolos.

Gwynllyw is credited as the founding father of the city of Newport, and the cathedral there is dedicated to him to this day. As a young man, he fell head over heels in love with Gwladys, the daughter of King Brychan (later Anglicised to Brecon). He wanted to marry her, but Brychan refused him. So Gwynllyw took an army of 300 men to knock on his castle gates and kidnapped her.

His passion for Gwladys never seemed to falter, even in old age. An account of his later life, after Gwynllyw had been converted to Christianity by his son Cadoc, tells that he sought a prayerful retreat on a desolate mountain. However, he could never stay up there for long, as he could not help himself from running back down the mountain to his wife's bed.

But he was hardly parent of the month. There is a story that one day, while out on a drinking spree, he gave the infant St Cadoc away to a total stranger in exchange for a cow. We've all done it. Oh no, hold on, we haven't, have we?

But against all the odds, Cadoc grew up to be a cornerstone of early Christian mission in northern Europe, and famous across the known world for his wisdom. In the modern Catholic church, he is still patron saint of burns and skin complaints. His father? Patron saint of Newport and pirates. No words needed.

St Cadoc

GATEWAYS TO THE UNDERWORLD

Across the counties of South Wales, there are many landmarks that are supposedly conduits to the other side. These beliefs are often a hangover from pagan times, when everything from streams to storms had a spirit or god associated with them.

Many of the tales in this chapter, however, ultimately stem from the Church, and were intended to deter ordinary people from pursuing pagan worship at traditional sites. I always find it fascinating that these stories have managed to survive for so long in popular superstition – in many cases, right up to the twentieth century.

It will probably come as no surprise that one such portal to the great beyond is the incredible neolithic burial chamber at Tinkin's Wood, between Dyffryn House and the village of St Nicholas. Historically speaking, there might not be a more significant site anywhere in the Vale of Glamorgan. It is believed to be 2,000 years older than Stonehenge, and its vast cap stone measures over twenty-four feet by fifteen feet, and is estimated to weigh a staggering forty tons.

The scale of the tomb begs the question, how on earth did people manage to build it? Let alone build it well enough for it still to be standing today?

Interestingly, evidence suggests that the tomb's builders were in fact the go-to burial chamber designers of their day – and not just locally, but throughout northern Europe. Identical structures built in the same period are to be found in Brittany and around the estuary of the Seine. People in the Stone Age led a much more nomadic existence than we do today. They followed the wild herds and seasons to where conditions were most convivial and food most abundant. So it is very likely that the people who built the burial chamber in Tinkin's Wood were the same as built the ones in northern France.

In later history, a lot of mystery surrounded this ancient place. No doubt it would have been revered by pagans, who would have gathered here on dates of ritual significance. In time, this would have made it a target for the early Christian church. So it is that we see stories warning that, if you were to spend a night at the tomb, during the Winter Solstice or the Summer Solstice or the Beltane, you would go mad – stories clearly designed to stamp out pagan rituals in a country that was slowly adopting Christianity.

However, in the eighteenth century, a bit late for Christian scare tactics, we have another interesting tale. At the time, there were three inns in St Nicholas, including the Three Tuns, which is now a large family house. (Its name comes from the heraldic arms of the Vintner's Guild of the City of London, but I digress.)

In our story, a chap had whiled away a few too many hours at the Three Tuns, and was now wending his way back through the lanes to his farm. He got as far as the burial chamber when he felt a need to relieve himself. As he did so, he felt a spirit grab him by the hair and lift him clean off the ground. He wriggled and struggled and called out for help, but the force was too strong to fight against.

Then he saw, opening up in front of him, a gateway to the spirit world, and from within it, tortured souls beckoning him to join them.

He kicked his legs to and fro, trying to resist, and somehow the force that had been carrying him lost its grip. He fell to the ground and ran into the night screaming.

Another known portal was a whirlpool to be found in the River Taff in Cardiff. It has now disappeared due to extensive flood prevention works and the permanent flooding of Cardiff Bay. It was once referred to as one of the seven wonders of Glamorgan.

People believed that this whirlpool was fathomless, and that in its cavernous depths lived a serpent who would gorge itself on any unfortunate victims sucked into its lair. If ever someone floated to the surface after being trapped in the whirlpool, it was believed that they must be virtuous, as the serpent would not touch those blessed by God. This applied whether or not the unfortunate individual was alive or dead.

It was also said that this whirlpool had a winch attached to it. That is not a misspelling of witch, nor is it anything to do with the sort of winch you might use to raise a heavy object.

Winches were characters in Welsh folklore similar to sirens or mermaids in ancient Greek mythology: alluring temptresses that lived in water and would entice unsuspecting male victims to their deaths. The Taff's winch was said to bathe near youths who fished or swam in the river. As they swam out to her, they would be caught in the swirling water and dragged to their deaths.

A winch making eyes

A teller of this tale to a nineteenth-century traveller described this winch as the devil in disguise. She said of the whirlpool, 'It reaches from the Taff to the mouth of perdition, where Satan waits for the souls who are beguiled by the lovely lady'.

A similar whirlpool can be found higher in the Taff, at Pontypridd; and another near the Nash, a sandbank in the Bristol Channel off the Vale Heritage Coast (near the aptly named Nash Point lighthouse). Similar legends are associated with both of them.

THE DROVER OF
CRAIG Y DINAS

In my chapter on the Ridgeway, I mentioned that some people believe Peterston-Super-Montum (or Llanbedr-ar-y-Mynydd in Welsh) to be the last resting place of King Arthur. But this is not the first such claim made in our area. I was delighted to discover a very old legend on the subject, possibly dating back to the thirteenth or fourteenth century. It begins with a drover from Craig-y-Dinas, in the Neath valley…

For thousands of years, drovers drove their livestock from the farms of West Wales to the markets of English cities, where they fetched the highest prices.

In our story, a drover from Craig-y-Dinas was taking the very familiar road home from Barnet Fair, after selling his charges at the market there. He paused for a moment to rest on London Bridge, leaning on his stout hazel staff. Tired from his long day, he decided to visit an eating house on the south bank, to build up his strength ready for the long walk home.

He was joined at his table by a slightly feral-looking stranger, with tangled hair and wild eyes. The stranger was transfixed by the drover's trusty staff.

'Where did you get this?' he asked excitedly.

'I cut it from a hazel tree near where I live,' the drover replied.

The stranger declared that the stick must have grown on a spot where treasures of metal, gold and silver could be found. He offered to make the drover the master of such treasures if he would take him to the spot where this hazel tree grew. This sounded like a good arrangement all round; the drover agreed, and the following morning (after they had celebrated their new pact) the two of them set off together.

The morning after their arrival at the drover's cottage, the pair walked to the grassy hollow where the hazel tree grew, and the drover showed the stranger the stump from which he had cut the stick to make his staff. The stranger looked around with eyes aflame and announced that he had seen this place in a dream, and that the treasures were to be found beneath that very tree. The drover fetched a pick and spade, and the two them set about uprooting the tree and digging out the soil underneath it.

They had been digging for some time, and the drover was beginning to doubt his newfound friend, when a swing of his pick was met with a shrill ring. They dug away the soil around this spot and discovered a very broad, flat stone. It took every shred of strength they had to lift it, but when they did, they discovered underneath it a flight of broken stone steps descending into the Bible-black darkness below. They both took a lantern and started their descent down the steps, which brought them to a corridor where a bell hung from the stone roof.

'Never touch that bell,' the stranger warned, 'or the consequences will be dreadful.'

They walked on until the corridor opened up into a vast

cavern, filled with sleeping warriors wearing shining armour, shields and unsheathed swords by their side. In the midst of these warriors a circle of twelve knights surrounded another figure. From his crown, it was clear that this central figure was a king. These men, too, were all asleep.

The stranger told the drover that the king was none other than King Arthur, and the other men all his knights and squires. They would sleep until the Black Eagle and the Golden Eagle should go to war. The clamour of the eagles' warfare would make the earth tremble and cause the bell to ring so loudly that the King Arthur and his warriors would awaken and go forth to destroy the enemies of 'Cymry', establishing the king's rule in Britain once again. But terrible would be the results if the king were ever woken by a false alarm.

In the midst of the space where the great king lay were separate piles of precious stones and precious metals. The stranger told the drover that he was at liberty to help himself but never to mix up the two. Before turning to ascend the stairs back into the sunlight above, the stranger turned to the drover one last time, to repeat his warning.

'Beware that you never touch that bell. But if by chance you do, one of the sleepers will lift his head and ask, "Is it day?" and in peril of your life you must answer, "It is not day; sleep thou on." '

Many times over the ensuing years, the drover would descend into the secret cavern to claim a handful of treasure, and he became extremely rich. Twice he chanced to accidentally touch the magic bell with his head, and on both occasions a warrior asked, 'Is this day?' and he replied, 'It is not day; sleep thou on.'

King Arthur's subterranean court

Then came a day when his greed had grown so great, he gathered a far greater haul than usual. Struggling with the weight of the load, he glanced against the bell, and a warrior rose to ask, 'Is this day?' In his excitement the drover did not hear him. Waking, the warrior saw the drover making his getaway, weighed down with the king's treasure, and gave chase.

The warrior quickly caught up with the drover, and angrily ripped the treasure from his arms, pulling him back down the stairs to give him a stern beating. The blows raining down, eventually the drover managed to wriggle free, and fearing for his life, ran with all haste to the surface, pursued by the warrior. When the drover reached the top of the stairs, he faltered, tripped and turned, terrified, to see his pursuer behind him. But to his no small relief, the warrior stopped at the top of the stairs and pulled the mighty stone back across the entrance, before retreating back down the stairs.

The drover never forgot the severity of the beating he received that day. He never went back to that grassy hollow again.

Here is a lesson in the nature of folklore. Once a bard or storyteller came up with a great story like this one, their counterparts would think, 'I'm having that.' That's how we get variations where the cavern in question is situated under Carreg Cennen castle in Carmarthenshire, and two versions where the sleeping king is Owain Glyndŵr, rather than King Arthur. One is set in Craig Ddu, Snowdonia, and the other on the banks of the Gironde River in south-west France.

But the one which really takes the biscuit was written by John Hogg in the nineteenth century, in which he had the nerve to relocate King Arthur and his sleeping warriors under the Tower of London, and rather than his waking to save 'Cymry', he was instead to save England, and only England! This version was popularised during the Blitz, and even became the subject of various poems.

But we cannot get too precious. There is a very old story pretty well identical to this one, apart from the name of the king and the country in which it is set, to be found in both Danish and Polish folklore.

And you've got to admit, however much we would like to lay claim to the great king, this story is rather farfetched. A Londoner engaging in conversation with a stranger? As if.

SHAPESHIFTERS AND
TRANSMOGRIFICATION

In Welsh folklore, there is no shortage of people able to morph into other forms. A flick through the pages of *The Mabinogion* can confirm that. There's the story of Blodenwedd, who transformed into an owl; Delilah, who transformed into an eagle; and Gilvaethy, who first turned into a deer, then a hog, then a wolf and finally back into a human.

In later folklore, too, there is no let up, with everything from gwyls to witches ready to change into animal form at the drop of a hat.

Notwithstanding this, in my research for this book, I was flabbergasted by the prevalence of tales of this practice in the Vale of Glamorgan. Sometimes, entire communities were believed to have been blighted.

For example, in the eighteenth century it was widely believed that the villages of Wenvoe and Cadoxton, near Barry, had a real problem with werewolves. This belief seems to derive from a story (the origins of which are difficult to date) in which a maiden from Cadoxton was betrothed to a young man who lived near Bear's Wood, in Wenvoe. After a year, he jilted his sweetheart and got engaged to another woman, leaving the sweet maiden utterly broken-hearted.

The poor girl's aunt was incensed by this betrayal, and made a pact with the devil to exact revenge on the young man. On the couples' wedding day, in secret she removed and twisted her girdle and laid it across the threshold of the newlyweds' home. The moment the married couple stepped over it, to enter their home for the first time as man and wife, the groom was turned into a werewolf. He ran, terrified, into the woods, leaving his distraught bride in floods of tears. So grief-stricken was she that she died within a year.

Spotted in the Cadoxton area

The antics of this werewolf were the scourge of local farmers. He gorged on their livestock, and the people of the surrounding villages lived in fear of his blood-curdling howls.

But the witch of Wenvoe, aunt of the werewolf's first betrothed, wasn't done with him yet. She still wished to re-unite the former lovers, and left an enchanted lambskin out to tempt the werewolf. When he bit into it, he was transformed back into his human form, and soon reunited with his first wife. But he had lived too long as a wolf, and he treated his former love terribly. So the witch of Wenvoe turned him back into a werewolf again.

Predictably, the husband-cum-werewolf was a bit miffed at this. He lashed out at the witch with his mighty claws and killed her. Now, with no one left to turn him back into human form again, he would live the life of a werewolf for the rest of his days. The villages of Cadoxton and Wenvoe were forever cursed by him, and he was known locally as 'the wild man of the woods'.

Werewolves crop up a lot in old Welsh stories. People whose eyebrows met over the bridge of their nose were frequently treated with suspicion, as this was believed to be a sure-fire way of identifying such a creature. In most old stories, a witch would be responsible for turning a local man into a werewolf. The pan-European tradition of treating unmarried women with suspicion was as prevalent here as anywhere else. It did sometimes go the other way though.

The village of Candleston used to lie between Merthyr Mawr and Tythegston, but these days has been lost to the sand dunes. But back when it was thriving, a Candleston inn keeper's wife had a bit of a reputation, keeping a string of lovers behind her husband's back. A wizard, seeking to punish her for her propensities, transformed her into a swan. Despite her indiscretions, the inn keeper loved his wife dearly and begged the wizard to turn her back. He refused, saying that she would turn back into human form in a year, by which time she would have learned the value of monogamy.

The inn keeper tied a blue ribbon to one of her wings, so that when she was swimming with the other swans in the estuary of the Ogmore river, he would know his beloved wife from the others. But one day, when she made advances on a male swan, his partner fought her off, and in the struggle that ensued, the ribbon was lost.

When all the swans flew south for the winter, he watched them departing, unable to stop them, or even to spot his wife amongst them to bid her farewell. He never found out where she had flown to, or whether she turned back to her previous human form. They were never united again.

But if the innkeeper had come to hear a certain other local tale, then his story might have had a different ending. This might be total coincidence, but I think I might know where his wife got to.

There is quite a well-known local story about a farmer on Barry Island. This was back in the sixteenth century, when the island was still physically detached from the mainland, before it had houses or fun fairs, and the whole island was farmland.

While working in a field above Whitmore Bay, he saw a beautiful swan alighting among the rocks. There she laid aside her feathers and wings, turned herself into a beautiful maiden and bathed in the waters. After a time she put back on her trappings of a swan and flew away.

The amazed farmer watched this repeated on several occasions. Then one day he lay in wait for the swan, and as soon as she was transformed and enjoying the water, he snuck to the water's edge, seized her swan garments and hid them.

When eventually she rose from her bathe, she spied the farmer. Unable to recast herself as a swan, she asked him if he knew where her garments were. He claimed ignorance.

He offered instead to fetch her some clothes from his mother's house, to save her dignity. This he did, and they walked along the beach together while he consoled her for the loss of her wings. As time passed, they got to know each other, fell in love and got married. For three years all was well. Then one day, by chance, he happened to leave open the oak chest where he had hidden her wings. Spotting them, she was enraged at the deception. However, over the years she had grown to love her husband, so striving to forgive him she said nothing about her discovery.

But having seen the wings, now all she could think about was the freedom of the skies and the life she had once lived. Then the day came when she heard her flock flying overhead. She could resist the call no more. She went back to the chest and put on her wings.

The farmer returned home from work that day to see his beautiful swan-like wife, her wings outstretched, slowly flying into the sunset. Her voice could be heard plaintively crying, 'Farewell.' The farmer so bitterly lamented his loss that he pined away and within a few months had died.

There is another version of this story, in which a man from Cadoxton and his friend from Rhoose find another two swan-ladies on Barry Island. Like the farmer, they marry these ladies, taking them back to their homes. However the Cadoxton swan-lady gets run over by a cart (being a swan she was unaware of the dangers of road traffic), while the one in Rhoose re-discovers her wings and takes to the skies. A nice detail of this version is that, after the swan-ladies are gone, the two husbands are left to raise their children alone, and they all have conspicuously long necks.

Foxes were another great favourite. There is wealth of folklore from the Vale of Glamorgan about foxes taking human form, or the other way around. We have stories of such creatures from right the way across the coast. They probably originate from a family of foxes somewhere on our coastline that evaded all attempts to trap or hunt them. Superstitious county folk concluded that, naturally, they were part fox, part human.

A belief was that they frequented the caves of local beaches, and as such, if a vagrant was spotted in the area with sand in his hair, it was customary to provide him with a good meal, lest he return as a fox to eat the children. Over time these tales grew arms and legs, and we ended up with a whole host of stories and characters.

For example, one old story tells of a very wily fox that lived in the woods above Porthkerry. She was known as Catti Cwm Ciddy. The story goes that Catti was once a fine lady from a great family but had been cursed by a jealous witch to prevent her from catching the eye of her betrothed. The curse forced her to take the form of a fox. It was considered very unlucky if you ever saw her and did not offer her food.

The legend of Catti Cwm Ciddy emerged from a part of the Vale of Glamorgan that at the time was Welsh-speaking. The tale provides us with another example of folklore being imported into English, with a very similar story to the above, only this time about a lady called Kate, featuring a similar curse. Poor Kate also had to live out her days as a fox – only this time in the woods of an English-speaking part of the Vale. Kate is, of course, the English versions of Catti.

The legacy of the English version of the story, which is set in Tresillian Woods between St Donats and Llantwit Major, is the naming of the cave on Tresillian Bay, above which these woods lie. You may remember the cave in question from our opening story, where they were the sight of a rather grisly execution. Ever since the heyday of Kate's legend, they have been known as Raynard's, or Reynolds Cave – both 'Raynard' and 'Reynold' are corruptions of the French word for fox, *'renarde'*.

The book of Taliesin is believed to be the oldest secular story book in British history, and it is riddled with stories like these. Despite Taliesin most likely being from Gwynedd, and therefore not exactly local, I am nonetheless happy to give up the last words on this subject to the great man himself.

His poetic words in the following passage show why these works are still so revered more than a thousand years after they were written.

'Gwyddno Garanhir asked Taliesin what he was? Be he a
   man or a beast or a spirit? And Taliesin replied:
"First I have been formed a comely person.
In the Court of Ceridwen I have done penance
Though little I was seen, placidly received
I was great on the floor of the place I was led.
I have been a prized defence, the sweet muse the cause
And by law without speech I have been liberated.
By a smiling black hag, when irritated
Dreadful her claim when pursued.
I have fled with vigour, I have fled as a frog
I have fled in the semblance of a crow scarcely finding rest

I have fled vehemently, I have fled as a chain
I have fled as a roe in an entangled thicket
I have fled as a wolf cub
I have fled as a wolf in the wilderness
I have fled as a thrush of portending language
I have fled as a fox, used to concurrent bounds of quirks
I have fled as a marten, which did not avail
I have fled as a squirrel, that vainly hides
I have fled as a stag's antler of ruddy course
I have fled as iron in a glowing fire
I have fled as a spearhead, of woe to such as has a wish for
    it
I have fled as a fierce bull bitterly fighting
I have fled as a bristly bear seen in a ravine
I have fled as a white grain of pure wheat
On the skirt of a hempen sheet entangled
That seemed the size of a mare's foal
That is filling like a ship on the waters
Into a dark leathern bag I was thrown
And on a boundless sea I was set adrift
Which was to me an omen of being tenderly nursed
And the lord God then set me at liberty." '

Not known for his straight answers, Taliesin.

THE LEGEND OF CASTELL COCH

This pseudo-medieval turreted castle, peeping over the trees on the cliff tops above the Taff Valley, lends itself to legends. Just from looking at it you would suspect there must be a couple knocking about. And thanks largely to the man who paid for the castle's renovation, John Crichton Stuart, Marquess of Bute, we have a belter.

In the twelfth century, this land was not subject to the English Crown. It was a Welsh lordship called Senghenydd, and the castle was one of the domains of its overlord, Ifor Bach.

In addition to the well-known history of Ifor Bach's descent into Cardiff, and his capture of the earl of Glamorgan, there is also this fantastic bit of folklore concerning his haul of treasure and how he protected it against theft – maybe a little too well.

Under the castle there is a tunnel which leads down a flight of steep stone steps to a huge cavern. At the other end of that cavern is a passage which leads all the way to Cardiff Castle. Here, Ifor kept a huge iron chest filled with precious stones.

To guard it, he had three huge eagles with fierce talons, their eyes deep set and burning red. They were chained to the chest, but with sufficient length on the chains to move around the cavern freely. If ever someone ventured near the entrance to the cave, from either direction, these birds would let out the most bloodcurdling shrieks, which quite terrified the villagers who lived near the castle.

When a guard dog just won't do

Many men sought to destroy these birds so they could get to the treasure, but the eagles were formidable and could not be approached by any stealth. Their vision had become so accustomed to the lack of natural light in their underground home that no one could hope to get near without attack.

As time went by, the legend of the eagles and the treasure fell into the realms of myth and was largely forgotten. Then in the eighteenth century, before the castle had been rebuilt, a gamekeeper and his wife took lodgings in one of the surviving rooms of its crumbling towers.

One night, the wife was disturbed by a sound and woke to see a gentleman wearing a ruff in the style of the early Stuarts. He looked pale and sorrowful and retreated behind a curtain. She rose from her bed and followed him until he came to a section of the castle wall where a lintel indicated the one-time location of an old doorway, long since walled up. The figure then walked through the wall where this door had once been and disappeared from sight.

The woman ran to her husband's chamber and woke him. She told him what she had witnessed, and he admitted that he had seen the gentlemen himself many years before, but never since.

The following day the husband went to the local inn and spoke to a friend who had taken lodgings at the castle in the past. He also remembered seeing the spectre, and again only once. The other men in the inn listening in on this story began to speculate amongst themselves. Maybe this man was the ghost of a Royalist who, before being killed in the Civil War, had hidden his worldly treasures in the walls of the castle to avoid having them stolen by his Roundhead assailants? One of the men remembered hearing a story of a man who had lived at the castle in the reign of King Charles I and found immeasurable riches. Maybe this was his ghost, returned to show where the treasure was hidden?

That evening, the men all went back to the castle, stopping along the way to pick up some tools. They chipped away at the mortar indicated by the apparition, and the stones came away easily, reinforcing their belief that the walling up of this doorway had been a rushed job, in response to an approaching enemy. Finally, enough stone had been moved to create a hole in the wall big enough for them to reach through with a lantern.

Through the darkness, they could make out that the doorway did not open onto a recess or even a room, but to a corridor, and what looked like the beginning of a stone staircase. They decided that it was getting late, and far too dark to continue any further, and agreed to meet up again the following morning, to open the doorway and investigate what lay on the other side.

That night neither the gamekeeper nor his wife slept a wink. The noises that emanated from the hole in the old walled up doorway were enough to wake the dead. They heard chains clanking, distant screams and screeching, and the sound of clawing and scratching.

When the other villagers arrived back at the castle the next day, they found the gamekeeper and his wife very shaken. She could barely stand up for the fear, and the game keeper himself announced, 'We have opened up a doorway to hell itself.'

But in the daylight, the hole was silent. The men exchanged glances with one another, had a stiff livener each, then pressed on, unblocking the doorway until the gap was big enough to fit through one by one. But before stepping through to investigate, they each returned to their homes to gather together whatever weapons they could find. They returned with a brace of knives, clubs, cutlasses and pistols, feeling sufficiently prepared to face whatever may lie on the other side of the wall.

Gingerly, they walked down the staircase, lanterns and torches flickering, until they came to a heavy wooden door. On the other side they could hear scratching. There was something down there. Something big!

One of the men eventually plucked up the courage to step forward and push open the door. As he did so he let off a shot from his pistol. The loud bang in such an enclosed space, made everybody's ears ring, and for a moment they were oblivious of any other sounds about them. Then through the darkness they saw red eyes reflecting their lanterns, and before they could react, they were set upon by the eagles. None of their efforts were sufficient to fight the creatures off, so they rallied together to heave the door shut once more, running back up the stairs to the castle.

They set to work replacing the stones in the old doorway, and the gamekeeper and his wife searched for the heaviest wardrobe they could find to place in front of it. From that day on, no one ever entertained the thought of opening up the doorway again.

There is a nice postscript to this legend, proof that no one is above embellishing a story. John Crichton Stuart, the Marquess of Bute, who owned both Cardiff Castle and Castell Coch, was a very keen antiquarian and historian. He liked nothing better than to entertain his guests with the above story, suggesting that he too had found the entrance to this cavern, only from the Cardiff end. He claimed to have marked the entrance to the passageway with the placement of a stone eagle. His guests, of course, would instantly think of the animal wall around Bute Park, commissioned by the Marquess himself.

The only problem? There isn't an eagle in the animal wall. Any treasure hunters would be confounded, no doubt much to the amusement of the Marquess, a man otherwise not known for his sense of humour.

*

The famous Castell Coch, near Tongwynlais, is not the only Castell Coch in the area. A small ruin, in a wood on the edge of the village of Welsh Saint Donats, also goes by this name. However, this one was probably never a proper castle; more than likely it was just a fortified manor house. However, it still warrants further discussion, on account of a rather mysterious occupant who inhabited it at the turn of the fifteenth century.

To be precise about its location, this second Castell Coch lies on a hill called Mynydd Coch, which is now largely covered in a forestry commission wood known as Coed y Marchog, which translates as Knights Wood. It takes its name from a mysterious hermit who lived there around 1412. He gave his name as Sion Goodfellow the Miner, but he had a swagger about him that suggested he was far better bred than he was letting on. He did not mix much with the locals but was frequently seen receiving visits from knights and nobility from outside the area. When he died, he was buried under the sanctus bell in Welsh St Donats Church.

So who was he really?

In truth he could have been any number of disgraced or displaced nobles, but given the wider goings on at this point in history, a story grew that he was Owain Glyndŵr himself. Historical records of what happened to Glyndŵr after 1412 are vague to say the least. Which is strange: he was such a huge figure, it is hard to believe that he just vanished into obscurity. In Wales he had gained almost mythical status in the eyes of his followers, and his enemies believed him to be a powerful wizard, capable of conjuring up tremendous storms to aid him in battle. If he had been killed, or captured and executed, we would most likely know about it, either from the celebrations of his enemies, or from his supporters' rallying around his martyrdom. It is most likely that he went into hiding somewhere.

There are lots of legends, from all around the UK, about mysterious new arrivals who turn out to be Owain Glyndŵr in disguise. There is one from Corwen, in North Wales (not much of a surprise, as this is near where he always lived); there is also the legend of Jack of Kent, about a man called Sion Kent, chaplain to the Scudamore family. But Iolo Morgannwg always favoured Sion Goodfellow of Castell Coch as the true rebel king. Who knows, maybe he was Glyndŵr? It is certainly more credible than massive 1000-year-old underground eagles.

THE WHITE LADIES
OF WEST ORCHARD
AND LLANTRISANT

If you're lucky enough to have read my first book on local folklore and legends (available at all quality outlets!) you will recall an account of the White Lady of Ewenny. Remember? The ghostly spectre that haunts the moors around Ewenny Priory, near Bridgend. Not to mention the other white lady who guards the buried treasure in the grounds of nearby Ogmore Castle.

Growing up fairly close to Ewenny, I was always aware of these stories. More recently, however, I have discovered that there are many white lady ghosts in Glamorgan. So many, in fact, that I can't even hope to cover the remainder here. The white ladies who have made the cut in this chapter elevated themselves above their competitors thanks to their compelling backstories. If any of their spectral sisters object, then they'll just have to put in a bit more effort to make the next volume. Stack some chairs or something. Show some initiative.

Just one of many white ladies that haunt the Vale of Glamorgan

Near the village of St Athan there are the remains of an ancient castle called West Norchete Castle – later corrupted to West Orchard. In a field nearby, a fine lady, slim and elegant and adorned in white silken robes, would be seen to rise from the mists in the early morning sun. Her story is a pitifully romantic one.

Many centuries ago, a daughter of the powerful De Clare family, the earls of Glamorgan, married Jasper Berkerolles. She was very beautiful and well-connected, and her marriage to Berkerolles made him the subject of much jealousy amongst his more unscrupulous friends.

Berkerolles and these dubious friends soon went overseas to fight in the Second Crusade, and the whole time they taunted him mercilessly, suggesting that, while he was away, his bride was being comforted by a rival, his neighbour Sir Gilbert D'Umphraville, of East Norchete Castle, known to be desired by many women.

At first, Berkerolles just ignored these taunts, but as time progressed and the ugliness of war opened his eyes to the darker side of human nature, he began to grow suspicious. Those suspicions ate away at him until he found himself completely consumed by them.

On his return from the war, he accused his wife of infidelity with Sir Gilbert D'Umphraville. She vainly protested her innocence, but the thought of her being with another man had so ravaged him that he had become deaf to reason. He condemned her to a terrible doom. In a field not far from the castle, Sir Jasper had dug a hole, and now his beautiful wife was thrown in and buried to her neck. With not so much as a crumb to eat nor even a drop of water to dampen her lips, she was to linger in misery through this living death, until the inevitable.

Her sister pleaded to be allowed to visit her. To this Sir Jasper agreed, on condition that no food or drink be conveyed to the condemned lady. And so every morning, as dawn broke, the sister would visit her. She would approach through the dew-soaked grass, wearing heavy, silken stockings which soaked up the water as she passed. She would then stand close enough for her sister to be able to suck the moisture out of the folds of cloth without arousing the suspicion of the on-looking guards. By this daily act, she was able to sustain her unfortunate sister for another ten days. But for all her devotion, it was not enough to save Lady Berkerolles, who died of malnutrition and exhaustion.

When Sir Jasper came sufficiently to his senses to realise his wife's innocence, it was too late, and he went quite mad with guilt and regret.

Even as recently as 1863, women milking the herds in the area frequently reported seeing this beautiful, forlorn white lady in the fields around West Orchard. She was described as wandering in circles around a specific spot – no doubt marking the place of her doom.

It is worth noting that, before she was married, Lady Berkerolles, as the daughter of an earl, had been a countess. In Welsh, a countess is known as Iarlles, which for centuries has been the name of a lane which runs near the field where the good lady was supposedly buried alive.

It wasn't just milkmaids who had to watch out for white ladies, however. One evening in Rhiwsaeson, near Llantrisant, a farm labourer was walking home from work when he was startled by a ghostly white lady appearing in the road before him. The apparition approached the man with some urgency and said, 'Your wife has given birth to a babe this day. Go and bring the boy to me at once, that I may be saved.' Naturally, the man was pretty shocked by this, but even more shocked when he got home to find that she had spoken the truth, and that his wife had just given birth to a baby boy.

Terrified by the white lady's motives for wanting his new-born son, he spoke to the village parson. The parson advised that he should have his son baptised before taking him out of the house, lest the boy die before he could return. The father agreed and the baptism went ahead post haste. The man then took his infant son to where he had encountered the white lady, only to find her sitting at the roadside, wringing her hands and weeping. He approached and asked her what was wrong. She replied that it had been a condition of her redemption that she receive a kiss from a new-born, un-christened child. Then she simply vanished.

Also from Llantrisant, there is a legend of a shepherd tending his flock on a hilltop. While shading behind a rock, he looked up to see a white lady walking past, scattering flowers as she went. He wandered over to where she had been walking, but she had vanished from sight. He bent down and picked up a few of the flowers she had dropped and wondered for a moment at their beauty. He took them home and placed them in a vase of water. When he woke the following morning, the flowers were gone, the vase filled instead with gold coins.

There is no record of what he said at this discovery, but I can venture a guess 'Tidy!' As I am sure we all would say in his place.

GWRACH-Y-RHIBYN –
THE HAG OF THE MISTS

There is a phenomenon who pops up often in Welsh folklore, and in particular across Glamorgan; she isn't quite a witch and she isn't quite a ghost. She is something somewhere in the middle, very similar to the Irish tradition of the banshee. Known as Gwrach-y-Rhibyn, she is described by many sources across the centuries. One, a book entitled *British Goblins*, published in 1880, has this to say:

> a monstrous Welsh spirit in the shape of a hideously ugly woman whose appearance is typically with unkempt hair and wizened, withered arms with leathery wings, long black teeth and pale corpse-like features. She approaches the window of a person about to die by night and calls their name, or travels invisibly beside them and utters her cry when they approach a stream or crossroads. She is sometimes depicted as washing her hands there.

Marie Trevelyan further researched the phenomenon in 1909,

speaking to people in the Vale of Glamorgan who told her that Gwrach-y-Rhibyn's choice of victims had a pattern: 'This night hag never troubles new families, only those whose ancestors have for long generations lived in the same place; in other words "old stock". '

But dig a little deeper, and you find that legends of the Gwrach-y-Rhibyn are much more varied and complex than simple portents of doom.

Her origins can be traced back to the earliest written records. A legend in *The Mabinogion* features beings with very similar characteristics, descendants of Don, the water spirit. However, these hideous screaming creatures, who could foretell fortunes, were not necessarily all women.

Then, in *the Book of Tailesin*, the story of Afagddu tells of the hideously ugly son of Ceridwen and Tegid Veol. To compensate Afagddu for his appearance, his mother boiled up a cauldron for a year and a day, to create a potion which gave Afagddu all the knowledge in the world, just from a drop on his fingertip.

In later history, we seem to move from legend to superstition to actual sightings. One of the most famous apparitions ties in with an earlier chapter of this book, which told the story of the death of the last Stradling of St Donats Castle. During the long and protracted legal battle that ensued after his death, the Tyrwhitt family, custodians of the castle, would let the castle to a series of tenants – none of whom truly cared for the it, thus beginning its decline.

A story from the early part of the nineteenth century tells of one such tenant family receiving an overnight guest. On his first night, the guest heard a moaning and wailing sound coming from close under his window. He described it as sounding like 'a woman in the greatest of agony'. He went to the window to look out and see what the cause was. When he got to the window, he was immediately alarmed by the sound of flapping wings against the lattice, and a rattling noise like the clatter of talons against the glass.

In the morning he told his hosts about the disturbance, and they informed him that it was the Gwrach-y-Rhibyn, who always frequented the castle, lamenting the death of the last of the Stradlings in the direct line. They said that sometimes this mysterious figure wandered through the empty and silent rooms of the disused part of the castle, and the sounds of her lamentations were 'enough to turn one's blood to ice'.

Not what you want to see lurking outside your window

Further accounts of this St Donats spectre describe her flying in the twilight of a November evening, traversing the whole village from one end to the other. Her robes and outstretched arms flowed against the wind, causing a great roaring noise. She was also once seen beating the boundaries of the whole estate, accompanied by black spirit hounds with red eyes and drooling fangs.

These apparitions seem to be very common in the great houses of the Vale of Glamorgan. Not a million miles away, another Gwrach-y-Rhibyn was said to haunt Beaupre Castle, during the occupancy of the Edmondes family. It was said that she had taken offence at the construction of New Beaupre. Another story describes her rising out of the River Thaw, wringing her hands and flapping her bat-like wings in the twilight. Many locals also saw her wailing and sobbing in the ruins of the old castle, lamenting its ruin in favour of its more fashionable replacement.

Further examples have been reported in the remains of the castle at Kenfig, the neighbouring Sker House, in the Old Plas in Llantwit Major, and at Cardiff Castle whenever a Marquess of Bute died. But in the case of Llanmihangel Plas, we have quite a unique example: a Gwrach-y-Rhibyn with a backstory.

This absolutely stunning example of a Tudor country manor house is tucked away in a lane between Llanblethian and Sigingstone. There has been a building on this site since at least the twelfth century, and some parts of the house still date back to that period (including an old prison cell in the cellar). However, the majority of what you see today was built by James Thomas between 1500 and 1540. It has been the home of many of the Vale's oldest families, and even once belonged to Humphrey Edwin, the mayor of London in 1697. It is still inhabited today.

The story I shall be focussing on, however, concerns a member of the Thomas family, who lived here at the turn of the fifteenth and sixteenth century. Her name was Eleanor Thomas, though she was known as Eleanor Ddu, meaning Black Eleanor. For whatever reason, the servants and local villagers were terrified of her, believing she was a witch in possession of dark magical powers. She came to an untimely death when she drowned in the small lake in front of the house. However, any villagers breathing a sigh of relief received a shock when, nearly thirty years after her death, Eleanor was seen rising out of the waters of the lake as the groaning spectre of a Gwrach-y-Rhibyn, lamenting her family's loss of the house.

Now it might be quite easy to dismiss these stories as the ramblings of superstitious country folk, with no formal education. But balance that against this last story.

William Wirt Sykes worked as a journalist at the American consulate in Cardiff, in the latter part of the nineteenth century. Hardly uneducated, and in all likelihood not one for the superstitions of a largely unfamiliar country.

All the same, William wrote a story about a man in Llandaff who was awoken at midnight by a terrible screeching sound. He ran to his window and looked out across the river, where he saw the unmistakable spectre of Gwrach-y-Rhibyn rise out of the river and float through the door of the Cow and Snuffers pub (which these days is an apartment block). He waited a while, but she did not return. The following morning, the news reached him that Llewelyn, the landlord of the Cow and Snuffers, had died during the night.

WHEN AN ILL
WIND BLOWS

We have explored in earlier chapters (and earlier books), how the pre-twentieth-century country folk of Glamorgan, much like their counterparts across Wales, had a curious approach to religion. They may have appeared to be pious Christians, but in reality, they never really let go of their pagan rituals. They kept the old religion running alongside the new one. Even when that new one was nearly 2,000 years old. They believed in water spirits and demons, tree sprites and forest dwellers; even the weather had its own set of deities and rituals.

Freak tornados, which are more common than you might think in some parts of Wales, certainly required some explanation. In the north they were believed to be caused by the eagles of Y Wylfa swirling in anger. In mid-Wales, they were caused by the devil convening a meeting of his demons on the Black Mountains. And here in Glamorgan, elves and fairies were at the heart of them.

We attributed strong winds with portents and predictions, even personalities. In pockets of the Vale, people regarded the wind as both hungry and thirsty. In eighteenth-century Wick, Marcross and Broughton, it was customary to throw a handful of barley-meal and a cup of milk into any gusting wind, in order to satiate its appetite and pacify it. And these are pretty windy places, in an area where trees grow tilting horizontally to the ground, in the direction of the prevailing westerly wind, rather than the straight up method used in other areas. A lot of barley meal and milk would have been needed!

We have quite a few strong-wind related superstitions: if a storm blew on New Year's Eve, it was an omen of a coming pestilence. A sudden gust flaring up from nowhere was a sign that, somewhere, a man had hanged himself. A howling wind foretold mischief.

On the flip side, a gentle southerly wind in the summer was believed to deliver good luck. When you felt it on your face for the first time, it was customary to make a wish; you would surely have it granted.

And now the storm-blast came, and he was tyrannous and strong…

When I was a small boy, my father would often repeat an old joke about predicting the local weather. I am sure it gets repeated across Wales, with an 'insert local landmark here'. 'If you can see the English coast from Southerndown,' he would say, 'it means it's going to rain. And if you can't see it, it's raining already.'

This wasn't just a punchline: local landmarks were used as barometers. Certainly, Flat and Steep Holms, islands southeast of Penarth, were employed in this way. If they looked close enough to touch, this was a predictor of a coming storm. If they were enveloped in a summer mist, a heat wave was on its way.

But in the 1700s, if you wanted to be sure of some good weather for the weekend, you just had to buy some. There were people happy to sell it to you, and Barry was full of them.

Most people back then, sailors and seafarers in particular, were extremely superstitious. And with good reason. Theirs was an extremely dangerous job; your fate lay in the hands of a favourable wind. This played into the hands of a small group of people who you might either call enterprising or unscrupulous, depending on your own moral compass. They would sell weather to sailors. I have found records of three such people operating in the Barry and the eastern Vale area in the eighteenth century.

The first was called Modryb Sina (Aunty Sina). If you were sailing out of Lavernock or Sully, she would sell you a fair wind, enough to fill your sails and give your vessel speed over the waves, but not enough to put you in danger. She must have been good, as it seems she peddled her wares for over twenty years.

But not quite as good as another chap who lived on Barry Island, Ewythr Dewi (or Uncle David). His weather was so in demand that he was known to sell it as far afield as Swansea, not only to local sailors.

Both of these people lived and worked in Welsh-speaking parts of the Vale, and therefore catered to Welsh-speaking sailors. But what if you were an English-speaking sailor? Have no fear, you were catered for by Bill O'Breaksea, who offered a similar service in Aberthaw. We cannot be sure precisely when he operated, as records of him are sketchy, but chances are it was around the same point in history as Aunty Sina and Uncle David, or even slightly earlier – when Aberthaw was in its boom years, trading with the merchants of Minehead and providing the people of Bristol with butter.

It wasn't always the sailors themselves in the market. Folklore tells us of the wives of drunken, slothful or abusive sailors who were more than happy to pay for a good storm the next time they put to sea. It was probably cheaper than a divorce. Like I said, depending on your moral compass.

We have some record of the particular rituals these people would observe when fulfilling customer orders. At this point in history, tricorn hats were popular with nautical folk. Stage one was normally to take out a compass, then to turn the hat so that the front 'corn' pointed in the direction you wanted the wind to blow. Another technique was to prick an egg with a pin to drain it of its whites and yolk, catch any bad weather in the egg, then seal it up with shoemakers' wax. The egg was then handed to the customer so they could release the bad weather again once the voyage was safely over, by breaking the egg.

REFERENCES

Folk-lore and Folk-stories of Wales, by Marie Trevelyan

The Garden of Wales, by Stewart Williams

Saints and Sailing Ships, by Stewart Williams

Vale of History, by Stewart Williams

History on My Doorstep, by Stewart Williams

Glamorgan Historian, by Stewart Williams

Bard of Liberty: The Political Radicalism of Iolo Morgannwg, by Geraint H Jenkins

Dr William Price: Wales' First Radical, by Dean Powell

The Hanged Man: A Story of Miracle, Memory, and Colonialism in the Middle Ages, by Robert Bartlett

The Itinerary in Wales of John Leland, by John Leland

Speed's Map of the County of Glamorganshire, 1610

Caradoc of Llancarfan, by J.S.P. Tatlock

Butler's Lives of the Saints, by Alban Butler

Wales and the Crusades, by Kathryn Hurlock

Excavations in Cowbridge 1977-88, Parkhouse and Evans, 1996

Roman and Medieval Wales, by CJ Arnold

Dictionary of Welsh Biography, https://biography.wales

A Topographical Dictionary of Wales, by Samuel Lewis

140

The Normans in Welsh History, by Huw Pryce
Society of Cymmrodorion, by G Peredur Jones
When Wales Was a Smuggler's Haven, by Phil Carradice
Llantwit Major – a Fifth-Century University, by A.C. Fryer
The Book of South Wales, the Wye and the Coast, by S.C. Hall
Owain Glyndŵr – Prince of Wales, by RR Davies
A Popular History of the Ancient British Church, by EJ Newell
Margaret Smith and her research into Stormy Down
Various local history societies and Facebook history forums
Notes on the history of Ewenny Priory, courtesy of Philip
    Morris

ABOUT THE AUTHOR

Graham Loveluck-Edwards is a writer, broadcaster and historian. He lives and works in the Vale of Glamorgan and specialises in Welsh history and legends. He is a regular columnist of the *Glamorgan Star* newspaper and the *Buddy* magazine, produces informative and entertaining videos on Welsh history on his YouTube channel @GrahamLoveluck, and hosts *History on Your Doorstep* on Bro Radio.

OTHER BOOKS BY THIS AUTHOR INCLUDE:
Legends and Folklore of Bridgend and the Vale
Historic Pubs of Wales

FUTURE RELEASES EXPECTED SOON INCLUDE:
Monia, Monica and Monique and *Why Santa Might Kill You*

To buy books directly from the author (at prices you will not find elsewhere), to read his blogs, or to get in touch, visit his official website:

www.grahamloveluckedwards.com